Finding the Successful Psychopath

By

Stephen Shepherd

W & B Publishers
USA

W & B Publishers
For information:
W & B Publishers
Post Office Box 193
Colfax, NC 27235
www.a-argusbooks.com
ISBN: 978-0- 6922641-3-3

Book Cover designed by Stephen Shepherd
Printed in the United States of America

DEDICATION

To my dear brother and best friend James.

And to the psychiatrist who gave license to the successful psychopath in my life without ever realizing who and what she was dealing with.

From the Author

The reason I wrote the book was twofold. It came out of a marriage that ended suddenly and very badly (for me, at least). The ending surprised me and I started to do research about inexplicable cruelty and remorselessness. I quickly came across the subject of psychopathy and found it incredibly interesting and also quite unsettled science, even within the psychiatric profession. Psychiatrists, Psychologists, Criminologists and Sociologists are all over the place on the definition and no one agrees on the definitive measure.

The developer of the current "gold standard" test (the PCL-R), Dr. Bob Hare, is all over the place himself, suggesting that only about one out of one hundred meets the cut-off score of the PCL-R but then writes the book, *Snakes in Suits,* about psychopaths all around us in business and academia. Psychologist Martha Stout wrote *The Sociopath Next Door* which is actually a treaty on psychopathy (two distinct conditions, according to Hare, but terms that are used interchangeably even by those in the business) and her claim is that it is common to about one in twenty-five in a given population.

So I sensed their own confusion and alarm about psychopaths and, even as they were illustrating and warning about something fairly common, they were quantifying it as something more rare. It occurred to me that the problem was that they had become institutionally committed to the legacy of studying subjects who were criminals and those committed to psychiatric facilities who all had sociopathic (rule-breaking) histories and now couldn't break free of that model to accommodate and define people who weren't sociopaths but met the

"Factor 1" PCL standard for egocentrism, grandiosity, manipulativeness, and lack of normal empathy and remorse. Hare suggests that they may be as common as one in ten. I'm sure you've known some of them.

Although I'd like to think that this may get the attention of the professionals in the field, this book is chiefly aimed at a lay audience. Basically, anyone interested in the subject. People should be warned about this phenomenon.

........S. Shepherd
July, 2014

CHAPTER ONE

Getting to Know the Successful
Psychopath

I loved Anne completely. For fifteen years.
It can be easier than it sounds. As long as
you don't know what you're doing.

Anne (not her real name) was the most charming woman you could hope to meet. Her smile captured me in a second. All of our friends went with her and, perhaps, believed many of the terrible lies she told about me, in spite of what they knew of me because it simply wasn't possible in their minds that she could be such a shameless and cruel liar.

And some of them knew that she had been a petty thief and had functionally abandoned her infant son to a live-in nanny to pursue after-work bar-hopping and casual, sometimes high-risk and abusive sexual relationships, (though they knew nothing about how that related to psychopath). At least, that was what she unabashedly told me, her new lover and husband, much like a young man might brag about his youthful conquests to his immature peers.

This is an analysis of the world of the successful psychopathy. The word "psychopath' has such a terrible connotation among the uninitiated that most like to (erroneously) describe psychopathic politicians and business people as "sociopaths." To be fair to all those who cringe at the word, the definition of the word and condition are far from settled science (more on that in Chapter 4) even among psychiatrists, psychologists, sociologists and criminologists.

But the word is generally understood by professional psychiatrists, psychologists and criminologists to mean an unusual deficit in normal human empathy and a shocking remorselessness at harm caused to others. Another set of attributes that are common to psychopaths (but not required) include unusual charm, compulsive lying, risk-taking and disorganization. Full-blown, clinical psychopaths also tend toward impulsive anti-social behavior. And they are far more common than almost any of us understand.

Anne achieved almost every single criteria on "The Psychopathy Checklist," either by observed behavior or direct admission. Though I am unaware of any juvenile delinquency (she never mentioned any) this is no doubt more common with males than women.

In *Almost a Psychopath* (Harvard University), Ronald Schouten, MD, JD, and James Silver, JD, write: "most of us tend to think of psychopaths as men. In part, this is because most of the research on psychopathy has focused on men who are in prison, not to mention that men are more likely to commit the sort of violent crimes that make headlines. But we should not ignore the substantial body of evidence from scientific research, the media and popular culture that tells us psychopathy is a very real phenomenon among women. Research also reveals that psychopathy may look different in men than in women…"

I'm also not aware of a pattern of pathological lying to me, although she could have been good enough at it that I didn't know about it, and I trusted her completely. One could look at someone spending her life pretending to be something she wasn't – a person experiencing normal empathy for others as living a lie. I had a long chat with a psychotherapist who thought that my definition of "pathological lying," basically the sort that was flagrant enough to be caught, was too restrictive. Perhaps it was. Or perhaps deceitfulness and insincerity are all that is necessary to make someone without normal empathy or remorse a Successful Psychopath.

However, here are some of the lies Anne started to tell about me when she decided that I was no longer of sufficient use to her: I wasn't really trying to find work (first to herself, to me, and then to others). From her TRO request: "[Stephen] is drinking excessively…has been verbally abusing me, my family and my friends for years…[he] started verbally abusing me more often in public…[he] verbally abused me in front of co-workers…his behavior became more intimidating and angry toward me…he was confrontational and angry…[he] sends abusive emails…Stephen Shepherd has been threatening to take his life on and off for over 4 years…he would either threaten to ride his motorcycle off a cliff or blow his brains out…many friends said they could no longer tolerate his behavior towards me and that they were uncomfortable and even frightened by him…[he] was violent towards me…"

Few of these lies could be told to family and friends (who knew better – none of them had ever seen me drunk or verbally abusive to them or to Anne and knew that I wasn't a violent person) to justify Anne ending the marriage with the man who they knew as a kind, loving and devoted husband (she frequently bragged to them about the many loving and considerate things I did for her) but were in a restraining order Anne used to gain exclusive control of our home and prevent me from ever again setting foot there.

While I can't know what lies Anne told to friends and family, including my Stepson (whom I helped raise from the age of eight – see Chapter 8; *Son of Successful Psychopath*), I know that they served an important purpose. Anne's persona was a carefully crafted and maintained façade that she has spent literally every moment of her life attending to (as is often said but overstated, living a lie). To turn me completely away from her she had to reveal herself as the cruel and remorseless psychopath she really was (though I'm now sure that she just thought that she was "different" from other people).

Nothing less could have caused me to give up on her but, once the deepest of her darkest secret was revealed, she had to eliminate any contact with those who knew us both, less someone else learn the truth of it. Pathological liar, perhaps. But calculating, deceitful, mercenary and remorseless liar, when push came to shove, no doubt.

In the end, it was her remorseless cruelty that saved me. Had I lost what I thought I had, what I thought we would share as long as we both lived, I doubt I could have recovered. I certainly wouldn't be writing a book about it months later. But I had actually lost nothing real, at best a comforting self-delusion, at worst a long, self-serving con job Anne had played on me. I lost being used and deceived by someone I loved, trusted and cared for.

In my research of psychopathy, I've learned that Successful Psychopaths may or may not have many of the traits listed in traditional psychopathy tests. In fact, there is no consensus about the exact symptom criteria for psychopathy, and no DSM diagnosis of "psychopathy," only the Hare Psychopathy Checklist and a rating of 30 or more on his 40-point scale. The one defining trait of all psychopaths is egocentrism and an absence of normal human empathy and remorselessness for any harm they do to others. Generally, they are thought to not experience most emotions as others do. Being a psychopath literally means never having to feel or say that you're sorry. Anne never did.

Very little has been written about Successful Psychopaths, particularly female, which part of the reason for this book. I suspect that one of the reasons that is true, and why what science that does exist suggests that psychopathy is approximately three to four times as common among men, is that female psychopaths are better at hiding what they are. Women, even women psychopaths, have a higher emotional intelligence than men, so are less likely to trip themselves up, even if they are pathological liars. Women, even relatively psychologically well-adjusted women, are simply better deceivers than men because they are usually taught from childhood to conceal certain facts about themselves, such as the nature of their own sexuality and bodily functions, in a way that boys aren't.

And men obviously can't – though perhaps would never dream to – fake sexual pleasure or orgasms (though men will often fake interest in conversation to get into a woman's pants; all day and half the night if necessary). So again, motive becomes the thing. Do women fake pleasure to make a man feel more sexually competent? Do they fake orgasms for the same reason or just to end the sex with men who aren't?

Some men out there may be saying, aha! That's my ex. Perhaps. If she took everything you owned, stole your dog and never spoke with you again because you kept leaving the toilet seat up or even had a gambling or drug addiction. But if you were cruel, physically abusive or she found out you were having a long-term affair with a neighbor or her sister, perhaps not. Some betrayals can lead to anger and revenge without psychopathy and deserve precious little sympathy. Even so, what we are looking for, as a sure sign of psychopathy, is a lifelong absence of empathy, self-sacrifice or remorse toward anyone.

At the end of the day, individual psychology is always the why of it (the motive), not the what. But, often, the what tells something about the why. Anne's unnecessary, quick and calculated cruelty towards someone so devoted, who had given her so much, who had never been cruel or disloyal to her, comprises the "tell" to her personality. Certainly, no woman with the least amount of human empathy, compassion and remorse could have inflicted such cruelty to a man who had helped raise her son, built two homes for her and paid their bills out of his earnings and inheritance for 16 years, without a serious deficit of empathy.

I never missed trying to make a Valentine's Day, birthday, Mother's Day, anniversary or Christmas something special. That always entailed multiple gifts, including something sentimental (as I alone perceived it, apparently) and something with precious stones (perhaps the only sentimental gift for Anne). I always brought her fresh flowers.

I tended to have to identify and sometimes purchase my own gifts, especially late in our relationship. She was always good with greeting cards. She did buy me one gift semi-regularly: clothing. I thought it was kind and considerate. Only later did I realize: "trophy husband." What good is a trophy unless it's well polished.

Besides, all she would have to have done was to say that the marriage was over and that she wanted me to leave. But that is not the way of the psychopath.

At a certain point, Anne claimed to blame me for my inability to find work, e.g., "if you wanted a job, you'd have a job." It's impossible to know whether or how much she believed this but it is entirely believable to me that this is what she convinced herself. Without empathy, it must be impossible to imagine devotion, no less any degree of selflessness. This is the real tragedy of psychopathy.

This coincided with her taking over the mortgage payments on our current home after seven years. Also, the fourth year of me not being able to find full-time work. We had moved four months before the beginning of the Great Recession to ground zero of the subsequent unemployment crisis with the unemployment rate steadily at something over 12%. In addition, I was a 51-year-old specialist in a field with close to zero local demand.

I was able to find some work as an independent contractor and a handful of interviews in related disciplines but those jobs all went to locals known to the employer. So I paid our mortgage and most of our household expenses out of an annuity I had inherited. Anne was doing contract work and attempting to run a business that eventually failed and, after a short bout of unemployment, landed a low-level sales job far beneath the executive sales career she had previously enjoyed.

Eventually, my money ran out and Anne's questions about my unemployment became more pointed. Needless to say, my despair at not being able to find more work, was not very painful for her. I was also suffering from sciatica from a ruptured disc, which made it painful to sit for any length of time so I was working, searching for work, eating and most anything else, standing up.

On the afternoon of my third epidural, on the way to surgery center, Anne announced that she had planned for us to take a "little" car trip afterward, about six-hours for a two-night stay at a coastal B&B she had booked. Did I mention that it was painful for me to sit (in her defense, her passenger seat reclined fully so I would only have to stare at the car ceiling for six hours). In any event, the ideal recovery after the epidural, which is essentially a steroid injected into the spine adjacent to the affected disc and is designed to shrink the tissue pressing on the exiting Sciatic nerve, is to do nothing that might undermine the efficacy of the epidural to do its job.

I said nothing to indicate that I was unwilling to go because to thwart the will of a psychopath is to invite disaster. In fact, I had learned over the years that any criticism, even in jest, or resistance to "the ways of Anne," was to invite a volcano of anger and cruel insults. To apologize or to flee were the only two strategies I ever discovered to relieve conflicts, reason was simply not an option. After the marriage broke up, my therapist suggested that I might have been overlooking a meaningful sign. Um, yeah.

Anne was playing the part of concerned wife, sitting with me while the IVs were being administered, explaining our postoperative plans to the surgeon, a wry and somewhat stoic man, as surgeons are wont to be. I watched his expression turn from uninterested, to bemused, to something akin to incredulous. He said something in response but I believe that he was at such a loss for words for how to confront such a plan; it was mostly unintelligible as he turned and quickly left the room.

Anne apparently got the message because, as we drove home, Anne announced that she had cancelled the trip. The announcement began with foul expletives involving body parts that you sit on and incest. I calmed things down by offering that we could book the trip for later in the month; it was mid-December and we had until the end of the year to use the booking. Yet, for some reason, the fight was rejoined once we got home and Anne announced that she was leaving to go stay with her friend who lived in the closest city, about an hour away.

She had said she was staying there numerous times since she got her new job. The friend was also a co-worker and her office was in the city so this facilitated early morning meetings, or so I was told. I had always trusted Anne implicitly but after learning about the psychopathy, I may have been far too trusting. But more about that later.

Then she did something that she never did before, she packed up our dog Max and his food and bowls in the car with her and left. This became a pattern over the next few weeks, over Christmas Eve and other nights. I seldom heard from her and when I did, it wasn't much. We had bought a cut Christmas tree earlier in the month and I had put it up and strung the lights and pulled down the ten or so boxes of decorations from the garage. By Christmas morning, the tree was adorned with the lights and a single ornament that my brother had sent to us as a gift, and a small pile of gifts for Anne.

On the Friday before New Year's Day, which was on a Sunday, Anne had, once again, packed up the dog and was headed out the door and, for once, I stopped her to ask if she had any intention of telling me where she was going. She informed me that she was going to the B&B she had booked earlier, six hours away, for the weekend. I had already told her, based on her treatment of me over Christmas that I thought that the marriage was over. At that moment, I was sure of it.

In the wee hours of New Year's morning I heard the phone ring inside the house. I remember that I was inside the garage. It eventually stopped. Then it started again. I remember going into the house and hearing someone outside say "he's got a gun." So I went inside and picked up the phone and heard a female voice on the other end. I remember that it was pleasant.

The next thing I remember, I was sitting on the front stoop of the house surrounded by

Sheriff's Deputies, having a not unpleasant conversation. I can't tell you much more about what had preceded that moment (or much of what happened thereafter), except that after a night of drinking heavily and taking pain medication, I had taken my 9mm out of the fire safe, loaded it and, from the garage (according to Anne), called to tell her that I wanted her to call the Sherriff to come to the house so that she wouldn't have to find me when she returned home. So, naturally, she hung up and called the Sherriff. And then she went back to bed. Or whatever she was doing prior to my desperate call.

And that was really only the beginning of Anne's deceit and remorseless cruelty toward me, once she decided that our twelve-year marriage (and fifteen year relationship) was no longer worth her while, when I could no longer pay her bills.

People with normal empathy probably shouldn't enter into relationships with psychopaths. It is the perfect, human, parasitic relationship. More perfectly humanly parasitic because, unlike a tick or a virus, it is at least semi-conscious on the part of the host. So, for the psychopath, it is perfect.

"The intense charm of people who have no conscience, a kind of inexplicable charisma, has been observed and commented on by countless victims, and by researchers who attempt to catalog the diagnostic signs of sociopathy. It is a potent characteristic."

-- Martha Stout, PhD.

CHAPTER TWO

What is (and isn't) Psychopathy?

Psychopathy is considered to be a personality disorder that is defined by certain personality traits and behaviors in four "domains": interpersonal, affective, lifestyle and antisocial. The interpersonal and affective traits which appear fixed and common to nearly all psychopaths are: superficial, grandiose, deceitful, lacks remorse, lacks empathy and doesn't accept responsibility. The lifestyle and antisocial traits, which are highly variable are: impulsive, lacks goals, is irresponsible, and may exhibit poor behavior controls, adolescent and/or adult antisocial behavior.

Psychopathy is not considered to be a mental disorder or disease by the psychiatric profession, chiefly because it is viewed as lacking serious problems of perception and is not characterized by constant or regular functional impairment or disability. Psychopaths are typically intelligent, insightful, apparently rational and generally functional. They are also usually charming and persuasive, manipulative and deceptive. Even psychiatric professionals are often fooled by their charming personalities, intelligence and social skills.

And, unlike with other mental illnesses, the psychopath feels no sense of discomfort about his condition. Quite the reverse, most psychopaths feel very good about themselves and, in fact, superior to most others. Generally lacking guilt, remorse, fear or anxiety, they typically find themselves before clinicians only because of incarceration or court order.

But, in reality, the clinical psychopath is deeply delusional, with grandiose views of himself, the near total ability to rationalize the harm he does to others, and is dangerously impulsive. A full-blown psychopath may impulsively lie, cheat, steal or even murder. The psychiatric profession essentially takes the psychopath's presentation of rationality and functionality at face value. Because of their apparent rationality, hiding a deeply disturbed (and disturbing) personality, the pioneer of psychopathy, Dr. Hervey Cleckley, titled his seminal book on psychopathy *The Mask of Sanity.*

In a sense, psychopathy exposes the professions of psychology and psychiatry as somewhat political, and wedded to definitions that have long since been called into question. In the DSM, disease is measured always in terms of social dysfunction, not necessarily in psychological wellbeing, Admittedly a hard thing to quantify, particularly to the lay public, no matter what may be suffered in the mind. And no matter what harm the psychopath may create for others in society (especially from the top echelons of society) and no matter what extreme delusion the psychopath may experience themselves, the mere appearance of social functionality is sufficient to avoid classification as a mental disorder in the psychiatric diagnostic manual.

However, when discovered, psychopaths may be permanently institutionalized (in prison or in psychiatric facilities) due to the irredeemable nature of their psychopathology because of their permanent lack of empathy or remorse, and the self-delusions and fully-rationalized anti-social behaviors and the corresponding hazard they present to society. Murderers who are diagnosed as psychopaths are more likely to be executed, due both to their apparent rationality and cold-bloodedness, unlike those convicted of "crimes of passion."

The psychologist who developed the PCL-R, or "Psychopathy Checklist," which is the most well-accepted diagnostic tool for psychopathy, is Dr. Robert Hare. He calls psychopathy "one of the first [personality disorders] to be described in the psychiatric literature…a personality disorder rooted in lying, manipulation, deceit, egocentricity, callousness, and other potentially destructive traits."

"Psychopaths are without conscience and capable of empathy, guilt, or loyalty to anyone but themselves." – Babiak, Hare, *Snakes in Suits.*

The DSM (*The Diagnostic and Statistical Manual of Mental Disorders*, published by the American Psychiatric Association) "equivalent" of psychopathy is called Antisocial Personality Disorder. However, many experts in psychopathy (including Dr. Hare) take issue with the DSM definition of Antisocial Personality Disorder due to its length and complexity, a reliance on a history of reported maladaptive behavior and because, "[s]pecifically, the DSM—III—R criteria exclude, or at least do not explicitly include, such characteristics as selfishness, egocentricity, callousness, manipulativeness, lack of empathy, and so forth." [*Psychopathy and the DSM—IV*

Criteria for Antisocial Personality Disorder; Hare, et al]

APD should not be confused with what is commonly referred to as sociopathy, though sufferers of APD and psychopaths are frequently called "sociopaths." Clinical psychologist, Martha Stout, author of the national bestseller, *The Sociopath Next Door,* uses the term sociopath to refer to those, "not having a conscience, none at all, no feelings of guilt or remorse no matter what you do, no limiting sense of concern for the wellbeing of strangers, friends or even family members."

Dr. Hare defines sociopathy as, "patterns of attitudes and behaviors that are considered antisocial by society at large, but are seen as normal or necessary by the subculture or social environment in which they developed. Sociopaths may have a well-developed conscience and a normal capacity for empathy, guilt, and loyalty, but their sense of right and wrong is based on the norms and expectations of their subculture or group. Many criminals might be described as sociopaths." – *Snakes in Suites.* And from a sociological and entomological perspective Dr. Hare's distinction makes sense. Sociopathy is mostly a disease of social rule-breaking, whereas psychopathy has an added element of abnormal individual perspective and personality.

So the lay public can certainly be forgiven for being confused about the actual meaning of these terms and using them interchangeably to mean someone without a conscience, empathy for others and the moral compass that the rest of us use to navigate our relationships, since psychologists regularly contradict each other over these concepts. Dr. Hare's distinction is both that it is the decided lack of empathy that makes a sociopath a psychopath and that sociopathic behaviors must be also be a strong factor in the diagnosis of psychopathy. We'll have to accept the fact that experts disagree about whether a sociopath is defined by a complete lack of conscience or a conscience that is distorted relative to the society at large.

To get into the weeds a bit for the purpose of why I lean toward one definition than the other, I tend to accept the term psychopathy to describe the underlying personality disorder of gross egocentrism and lack of empathy, even if the clinical definition includes antisocial behavior. Dr. Stout describes sociopathy essentially as a lack of conscience, which is a byproduct of emotional attachment, particularly the "love for someone or something." I don't disagree but, from looking at twin studies, brain imagery and the early onset and fixed nature of psychopathic traits – stark egocentrism and lack of empathy – it strikes me that these traits (whatever their cause) make love and conscience basically impossible for the psychopath. Egocentrism is the proverbial horse before the cart of lack of empathy and the absence of love and conscience.

Dr. Stout chooses the case study of a boy who becomes infatuated with killing frogs in new and gruesome ways for his own amusement, as an example of her prototypical beginning "sociopath," and then goes to the question of the lack of love and conscience. Indeed, the youthful torture of animals is a classic precursor to adult psychopathy. But I can assure Dr. Stout that even normal young men don't outgrow hunting and killing because they first develop some kind of love for or attachment to their prey. It is more often the sudden and painful discovery of animal suffering and loss of life of a wild animal to whom one has no real attachment at all. In other words, empathy, as a feature of other-centeredness, precedes love or conscience.

In addition, the psychiatric industry's habit of using the terms sociopath and sociopathy to more generally refer to a pattern of anti-social behaviors, and the criminal justice system's basic acceptance of the notion that those guilty of mere anti-social behaviors can be rehabilitated, makes that term confused for the purpose of describing the personality disorder at the root of psychopathy.

"As diagnosed by the DSM-III and the DSM-III-R, as well as by the recently published DSM-IV (1994), "antisocial personality disorder" refers primarily to a cluster of criminal and antisocial behaviors. The majority of criminals easily meet the criteria for such a diagnosis. "Psychopathy," on the other hand, is defined by a cluster of both personality traits and socially deviant behaviors. Most criminals are not psychopaths, and many of the individuals who manage to operate on the shady side of the law and remain out of prison are psychopaths." – Dr. Robert Hare, *Without Conscience.*

Most of us have seen past behavior, either by ourselves or by others close to us, that fall into one or more of the ASP behaviors but was not caused by a persistent disregard for social norms or a visible lack of empathy towards others. All that really need be present is, perhaps, some youthful recklessness, bad role models, a difficult or competitive job environment, a certain need for "high-octane" stimulation or just bad luck. That doesn't make anyone a psychopath or a sociopath (though a "pattern" of three or more of antisocial behaviors meets the technical definition of Antisocial Personality Disorder, according to the DSM-IV). And all human beings often lie and deceive, both to ourselves and to others.

The key to all-too-common "anti-social" behaviors is the power to rationalize, basically to tell ourselves what we want to hear. Robert Trivers, a Professor of Anthropology and Biological Sciences, posits in *The Folly of Fools, The Logic of Deceit and Self-Deception in Human Life,* that we all are biologically adapted to lie to ourselves and to others. He makes an inarguable case that we have the senses to give ourselves "an exquisitely detailed perception of the outside world [but] as soon as that information hits our brains, it often becomes biased and distorted, usually without conscious effort."

He goes on to argue that the reason we are so adapted, is to more effectively deceive others. From the biologist's perspective an adaptive trait, by definition, is successful because it has survived over successive generations. So, Trivers claims, the lie-to-ourselves trait has a purely biological survival benefit, the most compelling examples surround war-making and other self-serving predatory behaviors. But he also offers examples, such as the rationalization processes that lead to unintended disasters (such as mistakes made by pilots and engineers) that seem to undercut the survival rationale. There must be other, more complex psychological reasons behind some rationalizations that are difficult to explain purely through biological adaptive theory.

I would argue that we have psychological needs to deceive ourselves, for reasons that go beyond deceiving others or survival benefits. One of our most powerful psychological needs (even if poorly understood) is the need to see ourselves as essentially "good." This can be in the form of moral goodness or competence at one's job or, perhaps most importantly, as a good parent, offspring, or sibling.

History and criminology are replete with examples of people who appear to have some empathy and remorse yet have committed awful acts such as massive fraud, rape, murder, starting wars, etc., but who are able to rationalize why those acts were necessary and even why those acts may commend them.

As humans evolved, we developed important features that our animal ancestors didn't have. Perhaps our most critical psychological feature is self-awareness. And, with self-awareness come the powerful emotional drivers of shame and guilt. Most of the lies human beings tell ourselves are rationalizations – why we did or have to do what may or may not be in our own best interests or the best interests of others – that revolve around avoiding guilt and a sense of shame.

And one important "tell" for psychopathy that marks them as different than the rest of us, and an indication that belief in essential personal goodness may be more complex than a simple self-deception used to lie more effectively, is that the power of rationalization in the psychopath is observably stunted.

The psychopath has no empathy or remorse so he doesn't experience guilt or shame like the rest of us, only his needs and desires and the drive to fulfill them. So, throughout his life, he has no chance to practice all of the many guilt-driven rationalizations we of normal empathy engage in on a daily basis. If self-deception were purely about the ability to deceive others, the psychopath should have rationalization powers at least equal to match their other formidable deceptive skills – they are typically most accomplished and effective liars.

But question the criminal psychopath as to why they harmed someone and they will often try to change the subject, deny that any real harm was done or that they had anything to do with it and then, when pressed hard enough, explain why it was the victim's own fault, how they deserved what was done to them, or even why they actually benefited from it (or some combination of the above, sometimes all within moments of one another)! They are spectacularly unconvincing when called upon to explain themselves and their actions, compared to the non-psychopathic.

The rationalization process is thought to be the sub-conscious mind reconciling the observable truth of things (arguing, if you will) with the conscious mind that wants to hold a different viewpoint. Trivers: " ...the key to defining self-deception is that true information is preferentially excluded from consciousness and, if held at all, is held in varying degrees of unconsciousness. If the mind acts quickly enough, no version of the truth need be stored." Again, Trivers believes that this is solely for the purpose of deceiving others more effectively; I think that evidence exists that avoiding a personal sense of guilt and shame plays a large role in suppressing unpleasant truths from our conscious minds.

And lacking any sense of shame means that there's a much smaller price to pay for being caught in a lie. The rest of us may carry the shame and regret of being thought of as a liar for a lifetime.

And one practical reason for being honest is so that we don't have to worry about keeping our stories straight. Many psychopaths are compulsive liars so it may simply be too difficult to remember which lies they've told to whom, even if they were concerned about being found out. They are also emotionally shallow so attempting to explain their emotions or motives, which they don't really understand, sounds unconvincing to those who do.

In any event, does this mean that the subconscious mind of the psychopath works differently? Is it able to better compartmentalize the unwanted truths in a way that others are not? Or is it that, within a conscious mind that lacks any empathy, those otherwise uncomfortable truths simply don't matter? The answer would go a long way to telling us where in the mind empathy resides and about the entire construct of the subconscious and conscious mind.

There is evidence that the clinical psychopath doesn't process speech in the same way that non-psychopaths do, especially when listening to or trying to describe strong emotions. Psychopaths can also frequently go "off track" in their speech, veering from one subject to another seemingly at random.

I want to be perfectly clear that we've been talking about the clinical definition of psychopathy according to the PCL-R (and PCL-SV) and that the subject of this book is something other than clinical psychopathy. Even though psychopathy isn't listed in the DSM, it is widely recognized by the psychiatric profession. Robert Hare (and his colleagues) make clear that a diagnosis of clinical psychopathy can only be done by qualified professionals - psychologists and psychiatrists trained in the Psychopathy Checklist, usually in a clinical setting: "PCL-R assessments require the integration of information from interview, file, and collateral sources. Information from these various sources is rarely available unless someone is already in the mental health or criminal justice systems. Further, the scoring of items requires close adherence to the formal item descriptions contained in the manual," (*General Ronson Commentary, Society for the Scientific Study of Psychopathy*).

However, for the purposes of this book, the definition of the "successful psychopath" would not meet the Hare Psychopathy Checklist test. The "successful psychopath" is typically lacking in the outright criminal behavior and manifestly anti-social behaviors or the sort of compulsive lying that would lead to discovery. They don't necessarily test high on the impulse-control criteria (lifestyle and antisocial) of the Psychopathy Checklist and, therefore don't meet the "cut-off score" for psychopathy.

Successful Psychopaths have the self-control and are calculating enough to hide their essential egocentrism and lack of empathy or remorse. Perhaps that also means they have greater fear and less stress tolerance than the clinical psychopath. They may also tend toward the manipulativeness, deceitfulness and an almost infinite variety of other anti-social tendencies that may be found on the Psychopathy Checklist, but to lesser degrees.

As I mentioned, the science on the successful psychopath, particularly the successful female psychopath, is sparse at best. Among psychiatrists and psychologists, psychopathology is defined almost entirely by behavioral dysfunction. And I think it is fair to say that psychopathy is where the entire DSM model of dysfunctionality meets a psychopathology it cannot accommodate. Even more so for the successful psychopath.

Dr. Hare writes: "[d]imensionality may pose a problem for diagnosing or categorizing someone as a 'psychopath,' a problem shared by other clinical and medical conditions (e.g., anxiety, depression, hypertension, obesity) that often are described and treated as categorical but in fact may be dimensional. But, dimensionality does not preclude the use of "diagnostic" thresholds for making clinical decisions. With respect to psychopathy, a PCL-R threshold of 30 (out of 40) has proven useful for describing persons as psychopathic for research and applied purposes. Those with a 'heavy dose' of psychopathic features may pose serious personal, psychological, and financial difficulties for others. However, even those with a somewhat lower dose may present significant problems for those around them, just as those with blood pressure readings below an accepted threshold for hypertension may be at medical risk (*A Comment on Prevalence, The Wall Street Ten Percenters, 2012*)."

At the end of the day, the one key aspect that separates the "successful" psychopath from the clinical psychopath is impulse control. Those who can understand and refrain from exceeding the norms of social behavior can be full-blown psychopaths in other respects; more egocentric, manipulative, deceitful, callous (lack of empathy or remorse), yet still fail to meet the Hare criteria for clinical psychopathy. The entire point of the "successful" part of the successful psychopath is that they can live relatively normal lives that do not generally present a physical danger to themselves or those around them.

This is not merely a dimensional difference, this is a difference in kind. The impulse control aspects of the PCL-R (compulsive lying and other anti-social aspects), may test extremely low compared with other checklist criteria. So instead of the clinical psychopath who, more than likely, will eventually be exposed through their criminal and/or overt sociopathic conduct, you have another creature entirely.

It makes sense the clinical definition of psychopathy would factor in sociopathic behavior, since it was originally discovered and defined by examining deeply dysfunctional, institutionalized people, typically convicted criminals (both Cleckley and Hare studied and defined psychopathy based upon studying prison inmates).

Removing the empathy component from the sociopath doesn't necessarily change anything in terms of public safety, (though it may mean that the plain sociopath can be treated and reformed) but Dr. Hare and his colleagues noticed that certain prisoners were different: glib, remorseless and shameless in their seemingly compulsive lies. These inmates seemed relatively irre-deemable and had long criminal records and high rates of recidivism. It appears that it is unlikely to be able to ever teach psy-chopaths anything resembling normal hu-man empathy or remorse.

Dr. Hare's heroic efforts to explain psy-chopathy – he has authored a great deal of literature on the subject including two im-portant books, *Without Conscience* and *Snakes in Suits* – to the lay public have a clear purpose: "...if we can't spot them, we are doomed to be their victims, both as individuals and as a society." Although the successful psychopath is inherently less dangerous than the clinical psychopath, that also makes them even harder to spot. And there appear to be many, many more of them.

Adrian Raine, a professor of psychology and neuroscience in the University of Southern California College of Letters, Arts & Sciences, conducted a small-scale study of a random sample of men to determine if there were structural abnormalities in the hippocampus and corpus callosum portions of the brain. Not only did they find asymmetrical hippocampi in psychopaths but they also found that this abnormality was less than half as common in non-psychopaths and what he termed "successful psychopaths," those psychopaths who admitted to antisocial and/or illegal behaviors but who had not been caught. This may mean that these brain structures that "regulate fear detection and information processing" may be more functional in some psychopaths than others and allow "successful psychopaths" to avoid detection (Archives of General Psychiatry, November 2003). Maybe some of these psychopaths would get by Dr. Hare's test. It is mostly a self-reporting test, after all.

Sigmund Freud is the most famous (and perhaps most infamous) pioneer of psychoanalysis. Although some of his psychoanalytic theory reflected both the troubled time and place in which he lived (Victorian England) and the idiosyncrasies of his own personality, his concept of the three parts of the personality, the id, the ego and superego, are still considered groundbreaking. In Freud's construct, the id is the primitive, instinctual mind, acting according to the "pleasure principle," primarily sexual desire and the avoidance of pain and discomfort. The ego is the rational mind where perception, reason and decision-making reside. Freud's super-ego is the inner voice explaining right and wrong to the ego and inflicting fear of and guilt for perceived wrongdoing. So, one way to understand psychopathy, according to Freud's idea of the mind, is a marriage of the id (primitive desire) and ego (intellect) with an impaired or wholly absent super-ego (selflessness, empathy, conscience and remorse).

Psychopathy (clinical psychopathy, at least) appears to be hard-wired. Recent MRI studies show that psychopaths have structural brain differences from non-psychopaths. Most recently (May, 2012) a study, led by researchers at King's College London Institute of Psychiatry, showed "[a]reas of reduced gray matter volume in the temporal pole (above) and medial pre-frontal cortex (below) and areas of the brains of the psychopathic group of antiso-cial men." Past MRI studies have also in-dicated reduced connectivity between an area of prefrontal cortex and the amygdale, two areas that are believed to regulate emotion and social behavior.

Psychopathy is thought to have both nature and nurture components but appears to be based upon strong genetic predisposition. A large twin study by Dr. Essi Viding of the MRC Social, Genetic and Developmental Psychiatry Centre, within the Institute of Psychiatry, King's College London, showed a strong genetic origin for psychopathy. Interestingly, the 7-year-old twins who were the subjects of the study, didn't show strong genetic influence for anti-social behaviors in the absence of psychopathy. It was specifically the lack of empathy and remorse which was strongly hereditary, not simply anti-social behaviors.

"The parents of psychopaths can do little but stand by helplessly and watch their children tread a crooked path of self-absorbed gratification accompanied by a sense of omnipotence and entitlement...we have learned that elements of this personality disorder first become evident at a very early age." – Dr. Robert Hare

From the nurture standpoint, some psychologists believe that a failure to allow a child to emotionally bond with either parent or otherwise deny a child the opportunity to express his emotions, such as love or sorrow, increases the likelihood of developing into a psychopath, especially if a genetic predisposition exists.

Dr. Hare argues that plenty of children are neglected or even abused but don't grow up to be psychopaths and, conversely, plenty of psychopaths appear to have grown up in loving, supportive families. It is entirely possible that the failure to bond with a parent seen in some psychopaths is the product of the child's personality and no fault of the parent.

Not long ago a much-acclaimed cable drama was created. The premise of the show is that a middle-aged high school chemistry teacher learns that he has terminal cancer and decides to manufacture an extremely pure variety of crystal meth to cover the cost of his medical bills, funeral, and to leave a nest egg for his family. Certainly, this is the act of a man of pretty serious empathy, if not outright selflessness (he has just learned that he has six months to live and his concerns fall immediately to those who will be left behind). Over the course of the story, due to the criminal element he has to contend with, he becomes a manipulative liar and remorseless killer; a psychopath. The trouble is, (and I am very much a fan of the show) the premise is impossibly wrong.

Whether born or made, psychopaths are what they are by the time they are grown children or adolescents. No mature adult who has learned to appreciate how others feel, simply loses that understanding somewhere thereafter. If anything, young men who show sociopathic and some psychopathic tendencies (there are quite a frightening number of them) tend to mellow, if not actually learn to be more empathetic (or something like it) as they reach middle age. These are probably mostly examples of rationalized anti-social behaviors or personalities that were never really psychopathic.

Development issues aside, the $64,000 question then is what makes a psychopath a psychopath. Clearly, even according to Dr. Hare's definitions of APD, sociopathy and psychopathy, a plain APD or sociopath is someone who has something resembling normal human empathy. It is the gross egocentricity and absence of empathy and remorse that makes a person who exhibits sociopathic behaviors, a psychopath.

APD is considered to be much more common than psychopathy. Perhaps that is partly because people who are defined by anti-social behavior are more likely to be identified than people who have a personality disorder defined by greater egocentrism, deception and a dearth of empathy, but better impulse control, making them harder to spot.

Either way, my question to psychologists, and one of the questions posed by this book is: why isn't someone who doesn't necessarily exhibit strong antisocial behaviors, but who still shows a distinct lack of normal empathy and remorse, possessed of a serious personality disorder? In fact, isn't the egocentricity, shallow emotions, and lack of empathy and remorse the true personality disorder (that is mostly inherited and fixed) and the rest just a highly variable set of comorbid traits and behaviors (that can be at least partially the result of upbringing and experience)? We'll further explore the question of the prevalence of those who meet the PLC-R or PLC-SV "cut-off score" for psychopathy and those who don't but show a serious empathy deficit in Chapter Four of this book.

As one of *The Almost Effect* (Harvard University 2012) series of books published by Harvard Medical School, Ronald Schouten, MD, JD, and James Silver, JD, wrote *Almost a Psychopath*. Like the other books in the series, *Almost a Psychopath* explores psychopathy, "along a spectrum, with normal health and behavior at one end and the full-blown disorder at the other."

The title, *Almost a Psychopath*, carries with it the connotation that a real disorder doesn't quite exist. Obviously, I disagree. The authors write that: "the basics about true psychopaths (their intensely self-centered patterns of behavior, willingness to hurt or intimidate others to get what they want, and a distinct lack of empathy and conscience) as well as how clinicians identify them (by using the PCL-R and related instruments), it is time to turn our attention to people who are almost psychopaths. As you'll see, the different factors that characterize psychopathy can come together in an almost endless number of possible combinations to describe almost psychopaths." That I agree with.

What the authors then provide are examples of people who meet all or most of the psychological qualities that separate psychopaths from the rest of us – gross egocentricity, manipulativeness, deceit, and lack of empathy or remorse – and variable patterns of behavior related to those personalities. They are "almost" psychopaths only because they haven't engaged in the compulsive anti-social behaviors (or been caught doing so) that would put them over the threshold of the PCL-R and other, mostly antisocial measures used by most clinicians. In other words, they have the personality of a psychopath, they just act it out in more controlled and subtle ways.

University of Cambridge research psychologist Kevin Dutton recently published *The Wisdom of Psychopaths*, which suggests that psychopathy can be seen as a riches of virtue, leading to success! He writes, "[t]he problem with psychopaths isn't that they're chock-full of evil. Ironically, it's precisely the opposite: they have too much of a good thing." "There's evidence to suggest that, deep within the corridors of the brain, psychopathy and sainthood share secret neural office space."

Of course, this reveals that Dutton understands little about psychopathy, seeing it as a mere collection of traits and behaviors such as charm and self-confidence, rather than a personality disorder of gross egocentrism, callousness and lack of empathy that can lead to the calculated display of what he considers "a good thing." Simply put, confidence and charm derived from a well-adjusted personality, real, hard-won accomplishment and a genuine affection for people is quite different from that displayed for effect because of the desire to manipulate people toward purely selfish ends. Motive matters a great deal, both for the individual and for those with whom he interacts.

Those for whom every interaction is based entirely upon the egocentric, mercenary desire to use people without the slightest empathy or remorse are a different kind of animal than the rest of us. Psychopaths can't truly love, or be selfless, or altruistic, or generous, or considerate, or kind, or loyal, or compassionate, or concerned, or feel joy at someone else's happiness, or to see beauty for its own sake. They're simply chock-full of selfishness and practically barren of all of the good things human beings can be. And living totally within their immediate selfish desires, they can never be contented; which is what all people seek but the psychopath can never find.

"...in the end, just as the sociopath has no genuine relationship with other people, he has only a very tenuous one with himself."
– Martha Stout, PhD.

And, quite unlike people with compassion for others, psychopaths typically use their charm, intelligence, self-possession and fearlessness to wreak havoc and heartache in the lives of the people they encounter and society as a whole.

Although Dutton recognizes that there is such a thing as psychopaths who are able to avoid the compulsive and overt antisocial behaviors that would probably expose them (and meet the Hare Psychopathy Checklist), he calls this simply "functional psychopathy" which literally means, well, psychopathy. The psychiatric professional already grants the psychopath the presumption of functionality by virtue of refusing to categorize psychopathy as a mental illness. Those who are able to exceed the abilities of the PCL-R psychopath in following the rules of society and avoid detection but who still have a psychopathic egocentrism and dearth of empathy or remorse are, indeed, Successful Psychopaths.

CHAPTER THREE

About Empathy.

The American Heritage Medical Dictionary defines empathy as, "[d]irect identification with, understanding of, and vicarious experience of another person's situation, feelings, and motives."

Similar to the all too human characteristic of lying (to ourselves and to others), considering how fundamental and important it is to human behavior, it is almost shocking how little hard science has been conducted to investigate and understand the nature of empathy (and sympathy).

The entire concept of empathy is not even very old (introduced by psychologist Edward Titchener (1867-1927) and was originally an idea about our reaction to aesthetics and the natural world, rather than to each other. His contemporary, Theodor Lipps (1851-1914), argued for a more human-centered concept of empathy, one that allowed us to recognize each other as "minded creatures." Lipps also took the idea of empathy from one of simple imitation of the expressed emotions of others to a much deeper perception of people and things.

Lipps conception of empathy was criticized based on the problem that there is simply no way to know that what you may be perceiving as another's feelings is actually how they feel. From *The Stanford Encyclopedia of Philosophy*: "...while Lipps diagnoses the problem of the inference of analogy within the context of a Cartesian conception of the mind quite succinctly, he fails to explain how empathy is able to provide us with an epistemically sanctioned understanding of other minds or why our "feeling into" the other person's mind is more than a mere projection."

Obviously, I learned this the hard way. Emotions that I was fooled into believing that Anne was experiencing, like empathy itself, but also real love, sympathy, remorse, loyalty, etc., were mere projections of my own feelings onto her. So, at the end of the day, empathy is only as real as it mirrors the emotions of others and is, otherwise, self-delusion. Clearly, this puts one in a problematic psychological state and at a serious disadvantage in any kind of relationship with a psychopath (and they prey on that).

So true "empathy," the ability to know the emotions of others, is at best a happy coincidence. Otherwise, it's a ridiculous notion, really an impossibility as a general quality of normal human experience. Human minds are as complex and unique as fingerprints. So, even if we have suffered, our suffering is different from the suffering of another, even if caused by a nearly identical experience (the death of a spouse or child, or a bout with cancer). We simply cannot "know" or exactly experience the feelings of someone else.

So why do human beings have a concept of "empathy" and, relatedly, the real experience of sympathy at all? It has no overt, apparent benefit – it doesn't get you sex, a job, or money, or food, or shelter. It is often painful. Just think of how every tear-jerking philanthropic commercial for orphaned children or abused animals makes you feel (if you're not a psychopath). I've cried over phone company commercials.

The natural ability to understand and "feel" (be sympathetic with) the emotions of others – certainly has a nurture (the product of experience in life, rather than genetic makeup), component. But "empathy" seems so much the default nature of (non-psychopathic) humans, male or female, of any race, that this nurture aspect seems more like a process of unlearning how to be empathetic toward others. This suggests that there must also be a nature (genetic) component to human empathy (we're using the common usage of the term from here forward so no more scare quotes), so the origin of empathy must be very old (early Christians, living almost 2,000 years ago, suggested that we should be kind even to those who despise us and take care of the poor - perhaps an admonishment to practice empathy (or sympathy) as a means to save one's own soul) and have some adaptive benefit.

Selective adaptation is merely a process of a particular trait surviving because it favored survival. So empathy experienced by a mother over the hunger or fear of an off-spring may cause that off-spring to survive, causing that empathy trait to survive. Likewise, the empathy trait of a male concerning the fear of threat to the female mate, concern for which may help to cause the survival of the female and the inherited empathy trait of the male, and so on. So empathy may well have a basic, hard-wired, survival-of-the-fittest basis in human psychology. Perversely, the very unlikeliness of it, in the face of all of the disadvantages it presents, is evidence of its genetic basis.

Perhaps it is vestigial. Empathy may be a part of what's left of a sixth sense that is common to all advanced animal species. It may be an ability to sense the intentions of other like animals (they may have real empathy beyond their human cousin's sympathy), that humans have mostly lost through evolution and our focus on other senses during the development of the intellect, language, logic and visual expression, etc.

It has been shown by biologists and animal behaviorists that many animal species communicate intentions without speech (obviously). It is widely assumed, and in many cases rightly so, that this is through complex body language that is imperceptible to humans. But what if advanced animal species can "sense" the intentions of other animals through actual empathy? And what of cross-species sensing, such as animals seeming to know or "read" the intentions of humans in advance, if this is based merely upon body language. How do other species know human body language? Most humans don't.

As we've discussed, empathy is often confused and/or conflated with sympathy. And here's where things get interesting. It is actually sympathy, not empathy, which is implied by the definition of psychopathy. Remember, psychopathy is defined not by an inability to know the emotions of others but an inability to understand and identify with the emotions of others, i.e., "shallow emotions," in oneself (compared to the norm) and "not experienc[ing] any reciprocal emotion or sympathy."

The fact is, the word empathy, as it is universally used in the psychiatric profession with regards to psychopathy, is a misnomer. It can loosely be said that it refers to knowing, i.e., understanding, how others feel generally. And it is true that the psychopath cannot fully understand feelings that they can't experience as others do, such as real love, compassion, sympathy and remorse. On the other hand, psychopaths do appear to experience emotions such as anger, sadness, frustration, impatience, etc., albeit more shallowly than most.

So, when psychologists refer to the lack of empathy in psychopaths (or conscience in sociopaths), they are actually referring to the fact that psychopaths don't care how others feel, they have no sympathy or compassion for the feelings of others (especially negative feelings caused by the actions of the psychopath). Psychopathy isn't really defined by a relative inability to be empathetic – to actually know what others are feeling. Psychopaths are actually quite expert at figuring out how others feel, perhaps as much as any of us can guess what others are feelings, because they are constantly and opportunistically analyzing those around them because it helps them to manipulate others toward their own ends.

As Dr. Stout repeatedly points out in *The Sociopath Next Door,* they know us much better than we know them.

In a dictionary, under empathy, you will often find a notation such as, "[c]an be confused: empathy, sympathy (see synonym note at sympathy)." Too late. In the popular culture, even in psychology, empathy is commonly understood to mean sympathy for the suffering of others. Psychopathy is really the inability to be sympathetic to the suffering of others, particularly suffering caused by them, and the remorse (at least, rationalization) that would normally accompany such sympathetic suffering. Instead of worrying about "confusion" by the public-at-large, maybe it's time that dictionaries started adding a third line that defines empathy according to how most people have defined it for generations: "sympathy for the suffering of others."

So, for the rest of this book, no more scare quotes surrounding the word empathy. Just take it to mean what it means in psychiatry and popular understanding: sympathy, particularly for the suffering of others. Without the ability to appreciate the feelings of others there is no connection and no conscience, only the self.

Nevertheless, empathy towards our fellow human beings is hugely important, both morally and spiritually, especially from the Christian perspective. The idea of "turning the other cheek," and that you should "love your enemies, bless them that curse you, do good to them that hate you, and pray for them which despitefully use you, and persecute you," is manifestly and radically sympathetic, even 2,000 years after Christ's life, in our modern, "enlightened" culture. It is the exact opposite of the affective-deficient, successful psychopathic personality, that is constantly and ruthlessly "doing the math,' about what is in its own personal self-interest.

CHAPTER FOUR

Prevalence.

So what is the prevalence of Psychopathy in a given population? It depends entirely on how you measure psychopathy, which is much of what this book is about.

As it is, a great deal of the traditional work on psychopathy and Antisocial Personality Disorder, male or female, is from studies on those who have been dysfunctional enough to be ensnared by the criminal justice system or find themselves committed to a psychiatric hospital.

The *Hare Psychopathy Checklist* (The PCL-R) is the standard ratings tool used most often in forensic settings to assess psychopathy. A study by Dr. Hare and his colleagues suggests that perhaps one to two percent of the US population score high enough (as determined only by qualified clinicians using The PCL-R and case files) to possibly be considered to be psychopaths. Among "offenders," (convicted criminals) the proportion may be as high as 15%.

However, Dr. Hare's definition for psychopathy sets a high bar – 30 out of a maximum score of 40 across 20 separate criteria (such as "Lack of realistic, long-term goals," "Juvenile delinquency" and "Many short term marital relationships," "Pathological Lying," etc.) – for who meets the definition (cut-off score) of a psychopath (a score that is 5 points higher than what is considered sufficient to meet the diagnosis in the UK – so subjectivity is a feature of a diagnosis of psychopathy, even among psychologists).

Nevertheless, this is the definition for psychopathy. It is unlikely to be significantly changed or amended at this point and there may be good reasons to not consider doing so. Dr. Hare's psychopath, as defined by the PCL-R, is a very dangerous animal and probably irredeemably so.

He is self-absorbed, remorseless and prone to impulsive antisocial behaviors that are likely to harm others in nearly an infinite number of ways. And it is clear that Dr. Hare developed the Psychopathy Checklist expressly to help diagnose and identify the criminal psychopath so that prison psychologists and parole boards had the means to protect the rest of us from their predations.

But, for the purposes of looking at something similar to psychopathy but without the serious antisocial behaviors, if we were to narrow the test to only 3 of the 20 measures – say, glibness/superficial charm, callous/lack of empathy, and lack of remorse or guilt, one wonders how many could be counted as a less dysfunctional facsimile of a psychopath. Or, what if we were to eliminate only the impulse control criteria: pathological lying, poor behavior control, impulsivity, irresponsibility, juvenile delinquency, and early behavior problems, and adjust the score accordingly?

In *Snakes in Suites*, Dr. Hare and Dr. Paul Babiak write, "[w]e estimate that 1 percent of the population has a dose of psychopathic features heavy enough to warrant a designation of psychopathy. Perhaps another 10 percent or so fall into the gray zone, with sufficient psychopathic feature to be of concern to others..." Hare and Babiak don't say exactly what they mean by "gray zone,' or which "psychopathic features" they are referring to but, elsewhere, they say that "all" of those who test as psychopaths on their PCL-SV scale, "share the affective features of the disorder," i.e., lacks remorse, lacks empathy, doesn't accept responsibility (with interpersonal features, also marked by exceptional charm, manipulativeness and deceitfulness).

(Author's note: Dr. Hare declined to comment on what he meant by "gray zone" but it is safe to assume that those subjects met some, but not enough of the PCL-SV criteria for psychopathy. It is also safe to assume that, since the subjects in question had reached relative success in life, they had avoided the sort of anti-social behaviors that might put them afoul of the law and might test low enough on Factor 2 traits to avoid the cut-off score of the PCL-SV psychopath.)

Regardless, they are describing at least ten times the number of (professionally) diagnosable people, "with sufficient psychopathic feature to be of concern to others...," as many one out of every ten people you know (as opposed to one out of one hundred) or thirty million Americans. I think that getting our arms around this cohort is pretty important, regardless of whether they meet the clinical (non "gray area") definition of psychopathy.

"If I were unable to study psychopaths in prison, my next choice would very likely be a place like the Vancouver Stock Exchange." – Dr. Robert Hare, *Without Conscience.*

Clearly, what Dr. Hare is saying is that he believes that there are many psychopaths to be found in the well-appointed halls of businesses in the financial sector. Implicit in this assumption is the idea that there are psychopathic personalities who are functional enough to avoid exposing themselves through poor impulse control, including lack of discipline, pathological lying, and the sort of antisocial behaviors that would preclude one from the sort of high achievement that would propel one to the corridors of power and the pinnacles of society.

In his epilogue to *Without Conscience*, Dr. Hare writes that psychopathy, "is responsible for far more social distress and disruption than all other psychiatric disorders combined." That would seem to be an outsized effect for a personality disorder that affected a mere one percent of the population.

In fact, *Snakes in Suits, When Psychopaths Go to Work*, is an examination of the very phenomenon of the successful psychopath, one who is successful in business yet lacking in normal human empathy. According to Jon Ronson (*The Psychopath Test*), Hare is quick to point to presumed psychopaths almost everywhere in everyday life, "[a] lot of psychopaths become gatekeepers, concierges, security guards, masters of their own domains."

Dr. Stout puts the prevalence of sociopaths – those without a conscience, guilt or remorse – at four percent (one out of twenty-five). Her methodology is somewhat unclear (though her measures, such as the Minnesota Multiphasic Personality Inventory suggest sociopathic and other tendencies, rather than affective deficiencies, even more strongly than Hare's Psychopathy Checklist). Although she seems mostly concerned with the affective aspects in the Psychopathy Checklist, a lack of a discernible conscience, many of the examples she offers still exhibit overt antisocial (sociopathic) behaviors. And the prevalence of Anti-Social Personality Disorder more closely aligns with Dr. Stout's one out of twenty-five estimate.

Successful psychopaths are simply too socially functional (in our society) to even be classified as psychopaths according to the Hare checklist because they lack the impulsivity and serious antisocial behaviors to make the checklist's cut-off score. These folks are indeed stock traders, and CEOs, and lawyers, and even doctors. It is nearly impossible to conceive of them succeeding through the rigors of business, law or medical school, and still score highly enough on the Lifestyle and Antisocial areas of the PCL-R to test as a psychopath.

Remember, the clinical psychopath is prone to pathological lying, boredom, impulsivity, irresponsibility, poor behavior controls, sexual promiscuity and early behavioral problems, including juvenile delinquency. Doesn't exactly sound like people headed for summa cum laude or six to eight years of rigorous higher education, does it?

But what if you dialed back the impulse control characteristics to something close to normal and left only the "Factor 1" characteristics: glibness/superficial charm, grandiose sense of self-worth, cunning/manipulativeness, lack of remorse or guilt, emotional shallowness, callousness/lack of empathy, (non-compulsive/calculated) lying and not admitting responsibility for mistakes. I'm sure you can see where I'm going with this. If you haven't actually met anyone like this in business, politics or practicing law or medicine, at least you have probably seen them in action, their effect, and know they exist.

This form of pseudo-psychopathy is defined exactly by successful relationships (successful for the psychopath, at least), through effective interpersonal manipulation that is the byproduct of low-level empathy and remorse and self-serving deceit. Yet, simply put, it is not possible to classify successful psychopathy as a personality disorder according to the basic definition of the psychiatric profession; minimally a

30 (or 25) out of 40 points score on the 20-question PCL-R.

The test is, after all, a self-reporting diagnostic. If one were clever enough, a practiced liar (rather than a compulsive one) with adequate impulse control, could easily avoid a psychopathy cut-off score while still being bereft of empathy or remorse, perhaps far more dangerous and destructive than the out-of-control psychopath who is inevitable caught and institutionalized, because this person can wreak a lifetime of havoc (perhaps less physically dangerous) affecting many, many more people.

Dr. Paul Babiak, Dr. Hare's *Snakes in Suits* co-author, writes about an employee whom he identified as the possible source of a decline in productivity of a project team he was asked to work with: "[t]he individual came very close to the PCL-SV [a simpler screening tool for possible psychopathy than the PCL-R] cut score for psychopathy – a score much higher than expected even for most serious offenders," (presumably, he means convicted criminals here). "The PCL-SV also yields four sub-scores…that reflect psychopathic features in four areas: Interpersonal, Affective, lifestyle, and Antisocial. Known criminal psychopaths tend to score high on all four, while those like the reader score low on each one. The individual who caused such controversy on the team scored high on the first two factors and moderately on the other two. This profile indicated that he was grandiose, manipulative, deceptive, and lacking in empathy and concern for others, but also that he was less impulsive or overly antisocial than most psychopaths."

Naturally, he was less impulsive and antisocial than most clinically diagnosed psychopaths because the very definition of psychopathy includes a large component of impulsivity and antisocial behavior. The question is, how many of these people with sub-clinical psychopathy, but who still score very high on psychopathic traits, are out there living among us. And what are the proportions of those who don't make the cut because they are "less impulsive and overly antisocial," yet are marked by extreme egocentricity and a severe lack of empathy or remorse.

And, inasmuch that psychopathy has a genetic basis, it should have some of the general characteristics of other inherited traits. Depending on the number of genes behind a predisposition towards psychopathy (polygenic inheritance), you might see regression to the mean (a partial inheritance based on one parent's genetic makeup - the same way that one tall and one short parent tend to produce off-spring of intermediate height - or a normal distribution of psychopathic characteristics on a bell curve.

What this means and what the research shows is the distinct possibility that psychopathy isn't an either/or proposition but that people may have some combination of psychopathic traits in varying intensity. So it's easy to imagine that there are those who lack the some of the characteristics found on the Hare Checklist (or have a mild form of them), say poor impulse control, criminal behaviors and pathological lying, but are still very strong in the characteristics of egocentricity, manipulativeness, superficial charm and lack of empathy or remorse.

In 2010, Vanderbilt University's Joshua Buckholtz and David Zald conducted an experiment testing the dopamine reward system of psychopaths and controls. Dopamine is a brain chemical (a neurotransmitter) that is part of the brain's reward mechanism. A variety of highly addictive drugs, including stimulants such as cocaine and methamphetamine, act directly on the dopamine system. Bucholtz and Zald showed that, "people with high levels of psychopathic traits had almost four times the amount of dopamine released in response to amphetamine." They also tested the response to a promised monetary reward and found higher dopamine responses among the psychopaths and concluded that, "…because of these exaggerated dopamine responses, once they focus on the chance to get a reward, psychopaths are unable to alter their attention until they get what they're after...[i]t's not just that they don't appreciate the potential threat, but that the anticipation or motivation for reward overwhelms those concerns."

So it could be this dopamine response is what separates the clinical psychopath from the successful psychopath. In other words, it's possible that the successful psychopath may have the structural brain abnormalities discussed in chapter one that seem to hard-wire egocentricity and lack of empathy and remorse, but that the abnormal dopamine response that leads to impulsive reward-seeking is missing. Could this reward center anomaly also help to explain the psychopath's general fearlessness and low levels of anxiety?

Either way, one without empathy or remorse but with the self-control to hide it could do a great deal of real harm and is not someone you should want dating your daughter (or son) or running one of the country's largest banks (or the country itself). In the bestselling *The Psychopath*

Test, Ronson worries that "the madness business is filled with people like Tony, reduced to their maddest edges...people in the middle, getting over-labeled, becoming nothing more than a big splurge of madness in the minds of the people who benefit from it." That may be a valid concern, especially with certain childhood psychiatric diagnoses such as autism and bipolar disorder but, when it comes to psychopathy, a little bit goes a very long way.

In 1991, in the *Journal of Abnormal Psychology,* Robert Hare, Stephen Hart and Timothy Harpur (all of the University of British Columbia) complained about the DSM (Diagnostic and Statistical Manual of Mental Disorders) – III criteria for Antisocial Personality Disorder: "clinicians are generally forced to rely to a large extent on patients' memories and self-reports of their past conduct a state of affairs that is particularly problematic, given that untruthfulness is one of the disorder's symptoms... An obvious way to make the DSM—IV criteria for APD more accessible to its users, then, is merely to shorten and simplify the existing DSM—III—R criteria."

"The DSM approach to the diagnosis of APD is based on the assumption that personality traits are difficult to measure reliably and that it is easier to agree on the behaviors that typify a disorder than on the reasons why they occur (Robins, 1978, p. 256). Although the result has been a diagnostic category with good reliability, concerns have been expressed about its content- and construct-related validity, in particular, about its relation to clinical conceptions of psychopathy, in which inferences about affective and interpersonal processes have long played an important role."

The point here is that Antisocial Personality Disorder, the clinical disorder recognized by psychiatric professionals, is diagnosed based solely upon a set of specific behaviors. In other words, a personal history that must include certain events. This criteria set ignores the actual aspects of personality behind these behaviors and events, i.e., the actual psychology of the subject. They go on to describe what they call a "rather radical break with clinical tradition…[s]pecifically, the DSM—III—R criteria exclude, or at least do not explicitly include, such characteristics as selfishness, egocentricity, callousness, manipulativeness, lack of empathy, and so forth."

So, again, they complain that the clinical version of psychopathy, APD, ignores the psychopathic personality to focus solely on certain behaviors that indicate psychopathy, without ever really defining the underlying psychological disorder. Or, as Hare, et al, put it "the behavioral indicators do not provide adequate coverage of the construct they were designed to measure."

All this tells me that Hare and his colleagues are starting to question whether something like the personality disorder they identified as psychopathy is being grossly under-recognized by society at large. After all, how could a personality disorder that affects only two or three in a hundred people form the basis for the apparently widespread phenomenon described in *Snakes in Suites*?

At this point, they have had in-depth and longstanding exposure to a psychological maladaptation characterized primarily by lack of empathy and remorse (along with a highly-variable set of socially harmful conduct) that is being overlooked, and under-quantified due to a specific checklist of behaviors that may or may not describe every manifestation of psychopathy, for all practical purposes.

Before you think I'm making up my own definition of psychopathy, I suspect that most of those with the three measures just mentioned, superficial charm, lack of empathy, and lack of remorse, probably also test more strongly on the entire Hare scale – as Anne did. Add a high degree of cleverness, above average emotional intelligence (intelligence about other people's emotions, I mean), and a strong desire to not be discovered as an empathy-deficient, remorseless person, and who knows how many undiscovered psychopaths live among us. These are the successful psychopaths, those who are too clever and too motivated to not be discovered.

In *The Antisocial Personalities*, Dr. David T. Lykken writes: "[t]he full PCL, with the overtly criminal behavior items included, is clearly not an appropriate tool for identifying the 'successful psychopath,' the individual with the psychopathic personality who does not appear in prison populations because he manages to stay within the law or, at least, to avoid criminal conviction. One might use just the Factor 1 items of the PCL for this purpose although with some loss of reliability." He also points out that "[t]he two PCL factors correlate with one another only about .5 so that it is indeed quite possibly for someone to get a high score on one factor and a low score on the other."

Babiak and Hare answer an interviewer when he asks the question, "[w]hy aren't there any female psychopaths…?" The authors point out that, "the prevalence of psychopaths is almost as high [among female offenders] as it is among male offenders." But that there are important differences in how psychopathy is manifested by women and how these differences are perceived, even by psychologists."

"Thus, when a female and a male each exhibit a psychopathic pattern of core personality traits – grandiose, egocentric, selfish, irresponsible, manipulative, deceitful, emotionally shallow, callous, and lacking in empathy, remorse, and guilt – a clinician will often diagnose the male as a psychopath (or antisocial personality disorder) and the female as something else...the clinician expects psychopaths to be tough, dominant, and aggressive, and a woman who does not project these characteristics therefore is not a psychopath."

"Although the process of socialization fails to embed in the psyche of psychopaths the network of inner controls we refer to collectively as conscience, it nevertheless makes them aware of society's expectations about sex roles, about what is expected of them as men and women. More than most people, they effectively use these expectations as powerful tools for manipulation. So the female psychopath might make full use of the passive, warm, nurturing, and dependent sex role stereo-type in order to get what she wants out of others...[*Snakes in Suites*, 101-102]" I have to wonder if female psychopaths, like most women, have a higher emotional in-telligence that allows them to manipulate, and deceive, and avoid detection, in addi-tion to being responsive to social expecta-tions.

In fact, much of what diagnostic tests at-tempt to discover about psychopaths, ap-pears common to many highly functional members of society, maybe entire seg-ments of society – both the lowest and highest rungs. For that matter, who hasn't had a boss, or a friend, or even a family member who was superficially charming yet capable of cruel indifference to the suf-fering and/or harm done to someone they should care about.

And as I write this book, a new presidential candidate, who lies shamelessly about the current president, who bullied as a young man, who destroyed the livelihoods of hundreds, perhaps thousands, for personal enrichment, who can't seem to connect with strangers in an earnest fashion, who strapped his dog to the top of his car for hours at highway speeds, has nearly reached the pinnacle of societal success and power.

Of course, Dr. Hare would argue that it's impossible to reach a diagnosis of psychopathy in such a fashion but even Hare and other clinicians have examined the possibility that psychopathy may be overrepresented among the elites of business and industry [*Snakes in Suites, The Psychopath in the Boardroom,* etc.], as well as politics and the public media. That would explain quite a lot.

How many of Wall Street bankers, mortgage lenders, and futures traders (and the regulators and pundits who enabled them) who shamelessly ruined the lives of per-

Stephen Shepherd

haps hundreds of millions of innocent people around the globe meet the definition of empathy-deficiency by normal standards? How could many of them not?

And isn't it now even fair to ask if we aren't witnessing an enculturation (if not celebration) of psychopathy with reality television, from Survivor and Celebrity Apprentice to Reality Housewives, violent role-playing video games and Ultimate Fighting to, well, almost everywhere in popular culture?

In 2012 Labaton Sucharow, a legal firm specializing in anti-trust litigation, conducted a survey of 500 financial services professionals across the United States and United Kingdom. They found that 24 percent of respondents reported a belief that financial services professionals may need to engage in unethical or illegal conduct in order to be successful, while 26 percent of respondents indicated that they had observed or had firsthand knowledge of wrongdoing in the workplace. Even more troubling, they found that 16 percent of respondents reported that they would commit a crime—insider trading—if they could get away with it.

Of course, this doesn't prove a widespread lack of empathy among bankers. Nearly 40 percent of respondents believed that their competitors were, "likely to have engaged in illegal or unethical activity in order to be successful," and 30 percent reported that their compensation packages, "created pressure to compromise ethical standards or violate the law."

So there are systemic professional pressures in the industry to engage in unethical or even illegal practices. And everyone who has been awake since 2008 now realizes what tragic, monumental harm can be inflicted on people by the financial services and insurance industries, even when engaging in practices that were ostensibly legal and nominally ethical, like credit-default swaps. Likewise, mostly innocent and legal home-buying and rising property values, even over-leveraging them and ignoring the potential risks.

But, eventually, the society became enmeshed in nearly systemic selfish greed – basically, borrowing more than could be afforded to buy more than what was needed – that eventually fueled high-risk speculation and fraud by some home-buyers and predatory malfeasance by mortgage bankers, that lit the match to our over-fueled economy. That may not meet the definition of psychopathy (if it's even possible use that term to describe an entire society) but, clearly, no one was looking out for anyone but themselves, from top to bottom of the economic food chain.

In the end, however, real, remorseless psychopathy was shamelessly demonstrated by the thousands of super-wealthy plutocrats, who fought tooth-and-nail to avoid even a very modest increase in taxes on their spectacular wealth to help try to right the lives and futures they had played such a substantial role in overturning. They even complained bitterly about being even mildly criticized about it, just as any psychopath would.

CHAPTER FIVE

Finding the Successful Psychopath

I met Anne at our 20th high school reunion. I should say re-met. We were actually 6th grade sweethearts. Introduced to each other by our respective best friends as a relationship of convenience for group kissing sessions in the woods near our suburban homes (it was 1969). We laid in the leaves and swapped spit for hours. After several months of playing tonsil hockey with Anne, she unceremoniously informed me that she was no longer interested in continuing our relationship; the first but not that last time she would break my heart without the appearance of the slightest bit of remorse.

We went to the same middle school and high school, though we travelled in different social circles and never spoke again. Later in life her stories about this time described difficultly in achieving that popularity and, sometimes, even a sense of rejection. Her nappy hair was a constant struggle for her and for a time she wore a fall to conceal it. Her best friend had long, straight blond hair and was perhaps the most popular girl in junior and high school from the time she prematurely and bountifully blossomed.

At our reunion I was approached by a classmate, who was my brother's girlfriend during high school, and she reported that Anne had seen me across the ballroom and asked, "Whose husband is that?" Tell number 1: although we had been boyfriend and girlfriend and gone to school together for years, Anne forgot about me completely, including my name. Even as I approached her to (re)introduce myself, she remained clueless as to who I was. Of course, I had at least remained aware of her throughout our public school days and recognized her name as soon as I heard it. Our schools were not big enough to never see each other.

We went out with a group to have some drinks after the reunion and I took her home to her condo and slept on the couch. I met her 8-year-old son, Tony, the next morning and they drove me back to my car.

After several dates over a few months, Anne asked me to accompany her on a weekend business trip. We had a lot of fun together and a lot of fun sex. On our last night of the trip, after a day of fun sex, Anne tried and failed to bring me to orgasm again. She reacted with explosive anger. Tell number 2: psychopaths are extremely committed to getting their way. I was compelled to leave our room to escape her rage.

On the flight home, a flight attendant we were chatting with (on learning where I lived) asked if I could drop her where she was staying on my way home. When the young lady left us, Anne furiously made clear that I was not to do any such thing. After we reached Anne's house, she attacked me in a very pleasurable way and when I climaxed in her mouth she threw up her hands with a celebratory "yes!" Tell number 3: for Anne, sex was all about control.

Soon, I was spending most nights at her house, at first sleeping on the couch for the sake of appearances to her young son. By the following year the appearance had vanished and I had prepared my house for sale. In time, her episodes of rage became less and less frequent and we embarked on what was, for me, a mostly satisfying and loving life together. Together with her son and my deaf, epileptic Dalmatian, we took annual summer trips to the beaches of North Carolina. We flew to the mountain west to ski during New Year's or Easter holidays, took trips to several Caribbean islands, Mexico, Spain, Germany and Great Britain and visited with her longtime friends in New Jersey. Anne loved to travel and her work in the telecomm industry afforded us opportunities to mix business with pleasure.

After receiving discrimination settlement money from her previous employer, we bought a large spa and I built an 800 square foot deck around it with an arbor and hand-built lattice privacy screens and a large ornamental garden going up the hill from the deck. I landscaped and maintained the yard and did the household maintenance and repair, while we had other renovations such as new ceramic floors, kitchen cabinets and countertops contracted out. Though I shared the expenses, the house remained in Anne's name and I paid her "rent".

It was a Jekyll and Hyde experience, living with Anne. Long periods (eventually) of apparent sweetness, laughter, fun and sex, punctuated by explosions of violent, inexplicable anger. The explosions grew less frequent and less violent over time, presumably because Anne grew more and more aware of my trustworthiness, though she never really grew to trust me.

Anne was always planning her exit, even as we married. She insisted on a prenuptial agreement and had an ownership share written into the title of the house we bought together afterward, even as I paid the mortgage. While we lived in her house she held sole ownership and I wrote her monthly "rent."

We went to therapy together, she first and then me joining her at her insistence. We saw two different behaviorists. She sought validation while I tried to find some under-standing of and relief from her angry fits. When she had her blow-ups and I tried to reason with her she would always say, "It's not just me." Couples therapy was a way to prove it. Couples therapists typically don't take sides.

I came to love Tony as my own son and helped him with his homework, helped coach his baseball team, taught him swimming and skim-boarding, and we joined a nearby Karate school together.

When we put down Fletcher the Dalmatian at our home, born deaf and epileptic, finally almost blind and with a degenerative spine and hips, I cried like a child as I held his dead body in my arms. Anne went outside to our driveway to chat with and entertain the vet and vet tech. For the many months when Anne looked for work and worked from home, as long as I wasn't there, that dog spent every moment at her feet and otherwise lived with her for almost nine years.

As we travelled out west to ski, Anne and I started to talk about moving there one day. Within ten years we had bought a charming townhome in a small golf community about an hour from Lake Tahoe with plans to find a property for a custom home. We soon found a beautiful piece of land Anne coveted in a high-end, gated mountain community and, with money I had inherited when my father passed, put a down payment on it. In August of 2007, we moved across the country to our townhome with my plans for a custom home and dreams of finding more work. Then The Great Recession hit.

Within the space of a year, I had obtained only a meager amount of contracted work, a pro bono historic preservation client and interviewed for only a few full-time jobs. We had landed in ground zero of the recession in a poor rural county bleeding population near a city with the highest unemployment rate in the country. I spent the rest of my time doing home improvements, yard work, cooking Anne's meals and making her evening fire and serving on the condominium's board of directors, eventually as president. After about four years, I had spent the rest of my inheritance on our mortgage and household expenses and, as had always been my habit, generous gifts to Anne.

Anne and I also loved to motorcycle together. I had a standard triple when me met and, after twenty years of ownership, sold it to make way for new, very fast, sport touring machine. I joined a couple of online groups of young sport bike riders, some of them amateur racers, and was soon doing fast weekend rides on the rural, country roads that wound away from our home. Anne joined me on some of these rides and I was amazed how unflappable she was at the barely safe speeds and lean angles we took, near the front of the groups we rode with. Tell number 4: psychopaths are easily bored thrill-seekers who are seldom intimidated by relative risk-taking.

To my own naiveté, in nearly fifteen years with Anne, I never entirely recognized her gross egocentrism, deceptiveness, grandiosity, lack of empathy or remorse, or her sociopathic tendencies. In fact, I was propelled to study psychopathy seeking an explanation for Anne's unbelievable cruelty toward me when she decided that I no longer served her interests, after nearly 15 years of faithful love and devotion toward her every whim. Even an undergraduate degree in psychology failed to give me the tools to understand her in real time (I had one unit of Abnormal Psychology, which featured only DSM-approved psychological illness and variations of personality according to Meyers-Briggs classification).

The relevant tell here was one of Anne's favorite expressions: "[t]here are three sides to every story; his, hers and the truth." That should have revealed a great deal about what Anne believes about honesty in a love relationship as well as why she made up terrible lies about me to cut me off from my neighbors, friends and family (she boldly even tried to conscript my own brother). Only her story was to be heard.

Anne's favorite song was Tom Petty's *I Won't Back Down.* I think that speaks for itself. And the counselor I sought out after she ended our marriage was practically aghast when I told her that she frequently referred to me as her "trophy husband," in my presence. I had previously thought of it as a compliment.

Anne also liked to engage is some petty theft, both for items she coveted and probably for the sheer thrill of it. Small stuff, like restaurant salt mills and hotel ashtrays but, still, that should have been a red flag. Even more so, her apparent pride about it, even displayed to certain friends (who were not positively impressed).

Like many clinical psychopaths, Anne was poorly disciplined when it came to academic study. She flunked out of college her first year and read few books. She became a success in B2B sales, I think because it required little academic knowledge, only charm and the ability to manipulate others (though she was a quick study in the cursory technical knowledge of her industry, as long as she could have it explained to her verbally).

A sales profession also benefits from a strong desire to win, seeing every interaction as transactional in terms of one's goals. I suspect that successful psychopaths are overrepresented in sales, as in law, politics and medicine. I finally came to recognize Anne's habit of moving to a new job and immediately befriending the most useful administrative support staff, to navigate the company's politics and support her in the more mundane and disciplined of her tasks.

More seriously, Anne bragged to me about her high-risk sexual relationships and lifestyle after she left her first husband (two tells right there). It eventually occurred to me that she was stepping out after work for drinking and sex, leaving her tender young son in the care of a live-in nanny, instead of going home to him. That poor kid never stood a chance (see *Son of the Successful Psychopath*, CH6).

Anne also liked to brag about weekends with the girls, where they all assumed fake personas to mess with the heads of the men they met. She seemed quite enamored with herself and her elaborate portrayal of "Nicke Rouché" and how successfully she believed that she fooled them. I have no knowledge of infidelity by Anne but boredom, promiscuousness and risk taking are common features of any psychopath. And she travelled alone many times.

Anne had a simple life motto, which I mistakenly took as something she said tongue-in-cheek (but which she said often enough that I should have known better): "[i]s the fucking you're getting worth the fucking your getting?" It turns out that she had a hard, cold view of love relationships and applied this mercenary but ultimately pragmatic bit of math to all of her relationships.

"The philosophy of life that [psychopaths] espouse usually is banal, sophomoric, and devoid of the detail that enriches the lives of normal adults." – Dr. Robert Hare, *Without Conscience.*

I never missed a birthday, anniversary, Valentine's Day, or holiday. I used to buy cards and presents from Tony for Mother's Day. I always brought her fresh flowers.

Finally, Anne coldly rejected the man who had loved, cared, and worked his ass off for her for fifteen years. That would be one thing. People fall out of love all of the time and, under the circumstances, that simple falling-out would be entirely understandable.

But Anne mentally tortured him, stole from him, lied to him, and slandered his reputation to nearly everyone he knew and loved, to justify her own selfish cruelty. All because she decided he was no longer useful to her and she no longer owned and controlled him. Worst of all, he had discovered the truth about her carefully crafted image of normal human kindness and empathy.

The unpleasant fact is, happy endings are what we all long for but they are practically nonexistent. And practically impossible with the successful psychopath.

CHAPTER SIX

Son of the Successful Psychopath

As we discussed earlier, psychopathic traits, particularly Factor 1 traits, appear to have both inherited and learned origins. They are nature and/or nurture.

As we also explained, Anne's son Tony was the product of a bad marriage at a very early age and had, at best, a sometimes absent mother. On occasion, he called her "psycho."

Like his mother, Tony was extremely charming and also poorly self-disciplined. As a boy, Tony was nothing less than a wunderkind in his social relationships. He seemed to truly enjoy the company of his peers, younger children, and charmed the pants off of parents, teachers, even me, all of the adults in his like. Safe to say, he schmoozed his way through school and life itself.

Even though he attended one of the top magnet schools in our hyper-achieving mid-Atlantic state, where most of his friends and high school classmates were acing college-level courses, we literally didn't know if he would be the one student who didn't receive a diploma at his high school graduation ceremony. The trouble was, no amount of encouragement, help or prodding could instigate Tony to do his homework and assignments required by his courses, regardless of his intelligence or smarts. The one exception was his mock trial course which offered the competitive challenge that unleashed his skills in discipline, writing and follow-through like nothing he has faced before.

One early window into Tony's personality stands out to me. By the time I met Tony, I had already begun to mentor an at-risk young man, about Tony's age, as part of a local program I became involved with. I invited Tony to a park outing with that boy and, unlike any subsequent behavior over the rest of his entire childhood, he sat himself right in my lap and drew my arm around him, practically declaring his ownership and territory.

Tony was prone to hypochondria his entire childhood. Self-diagnosed aneurisms were the order of the day, even in his early years. Like a first-year med student, every injury or illness was grave; even life threatening. Even as a young man, a sprained neck from a snowboard fall was a hangman's fracture. He could be talked down from outright fear but it took a lot of persuasion.

Although lying and lack of self-discipline are typical of young men, Tony took it to high art. For many years, in spite of Anne and my best efforts, Tony couldn't be made to do schoolwork that would have been easier to do than to avoid. Though avoid it he did, concealing and lying about what he was required to do and concealing his failure to do it. It was often impossible to find visible floor in his bedroom.

In fact, Tony was a virtual textbook of lack of self-discipline. Though Tony excelled at sports and other ventures that offered highly disciplined environments, he was unable to do much of anything that required planning and follow-through. His possessions were often lost or destroyed. Even his cars and trucks, where I spent so much of my time, energy and money in my youth, often went unrepaired or maintained.

When we left our home to move west, we left Tony with a pristine split-level colonial house, with a magnificent deck, spa and yard, thousands of dollars worth of audio equipment and a 50" plasma television. Within a few years it was all lost or destroyed.

In his senior year in high school, perhaps sensing his academic failure and need for structure and thrills, Tony asked Anne and I for permission to join the Marine Corp. It

was the height of Afghanistan and the beginning of Iraq, so we declined. He had
actually gone to a recruiter on his own but
only our refusal to give permission to him
as a minor probably saved his life.

What saved Tony was his entry into the
closest volunteer firefighting unit. It pro-
vided exactly the top-down structural discipline he needed and thrived in. He was
awarded firefighter of the year that first
year and the county fire service immediately offered him an appointment to the fire
service academy.

Naturally, in retrospect, Tony pursued
Special Operations, receiving training in
water rescue and Hazmat of all kinds. Before he was twenty years of age, he was
witnessing death and serious injury and
cutting accident victims from cars. He
worked for an ambulance service, taking
the sick and infirmed to hospitals. He was
seeing pain and loss that I can't even begin
to imagine, to no apparent effect.

In fact, during my last visit with him Tony
unabashedly, perhaps even proudly, ex-

pressed a genuine desire for a major cata-clysmic local event to test his training and abilities. Despite my shock, I tried to explain that that would mean death and pain on a massive scale. He was unfazed and unapologetic. He even offered a wry smile.

Tony always had a very high opinion of himself. His success at sports (even though he couldn't move past the junior high school level) and the fire service created a cock-sure attitude and self-congratulatory belief in his accomplishments and abilities. Perhaps they were well-earned but, considering his own many failures and shortcomings, they seemed out of place. Even for a young man.

I never saw Tony cry, except over his own suffering and fear. Not over the death of his dog, the death of my father, or the death of his own grandmother. And he was never able to form a love relationship, even though he was handsome, charming and popular. By the time I was Tony's age when we left, I had had three, long-term committed relationships and was living with a young woman. I never knew why. Perhaps he was incapable of real love or was simply wiser about women and relationships than his romantic stepfather.

In the end, when Anne turned on me, Tony did the same, in the same cold, remorseless fashion. Our fifteen years together, my kindness, teaching and mentoring didn't matter in the slightest. Neither did my feelings or attempts to reach out to him.

If Tony really is deficient in empathy and remorse, he isn't at fault. Our personalities are shaped by our genes and early experience, over which we have no control. The idea that we control who we become is a fiction created by others. Tony had everything going for him, the love and devotion of those around him, all the moral guidance and material comforts one could hope for. It appears that it was insufficient to overcome what he was.

CHAPTER SEVEN

Silly rabbit, tricks are for ids

I apologize to you now, dear reader, for the tongue-in-cheek nature of the jacket art of this book and even its title. However, there is a point to it.

Obviously, the cover is a nod to Glen Close's excellent portrayal of successful psychopath Alex Forest, in *Fatal Attraction*. And there have been many, many portrayals of successful psychopaths in movies and television from male (Charles Boyer as Gregory Anton in *Gaslight*) to female (Vivien Leigh as Scarlet O'Hara in *Gone with the Wind*). Actually, the frequency of psychopaths in popular entertainment make one wonder why we don't see the possibility that we may be dealing with one or more successful psychopaths at any given time. Quentin Tarantino has described enough psychopaths to fill a prison. Blues music portrays more than a few. Heath Ledger's Joker was a masterful (if occasionally cartoonist) portrayal of pure psychopathy.

Remember Alec Baldwin's portrayal of "I am God," surgeon Jed Hill in *Malice*. Now that's a grandiose sense of self. And, considering the necessary pain one must inflict, surgery seems like a good place to land for someone with little or no empathy.

The actor Lawrence Tierney practically made a career of playing psychopathic personalities, beginning with "Sam" "... a psychotic murderer" (according to one reviewer) in *Born to Kill*, a post WWII film noir. The character actually displayed few psychotic behaviors (delusions, hallucinations, depression, etc.), probably reflecting the widespread lack of understanding about most mental disorders, particularly psychopathy. Sam was actually clever, egocentric, grandiose, possessive, suspicious, deceptive, manipulative and murderously sociopathic (all while mostly fooling and projecting his bad motives on those around him). In other words, he was a full-blown PCL psychopath.

The truth is, we actually love our psychopaths in books and popular entertainment. It's interesting that, at the same time, we tend to overlook them in real life. Though, in real life, we don't often get to see the scenes that reveal what they are. And, then, there's the charm. Except for psychopaths, most of us are suckers for the charm.

Now think of all the serial killers, drug kingpins, embezzlers, corrupt business leaders, school and church leaders who sanctioned the sexual abuse of children. Granted, some of them are full-blown clinical psychopaths who were clever enough to not be caught (this is not good news).

As of 2010, FBI statistics show that something like 6,000 murders go unsolved every year. That's nearly one unsolved murder for every 50,000 people.

The overall violent crime rate (which includes rape or sexual assault, robbery, aggravated and simple assault) in 2013 was 2.61% in the US. Some of these may have been crimes of passion or the out-of-control acts of sociopaths, not the cold-blooded acts of a psychopath, but that is still more than twice the reported rate of clinical psychopathy. And fully half of all violent crimes go unreported.

The facts and data show that many of us are likely to know, love or be tempted to love a successful psychopath at some point in our lives. Should we meet one under the right circumstances, we will likely find them attractive, smart, charming and engaging. And they are capable and willing to weave whatever tale they believe might interest or entice us.

And psychopaths, successful or not, prey on those with more normal empathy and remorse. Those who are the least likely to recognize what they are while we project our own feelings of empathy and compassion on them. But, for your own protection, should you become convinced that you are involved with a psychopath in any way; lover, friend, employer, even an acquaintance, your smart course of action is to run. Separate yourself as fast and completely as is practicable from that person.

But beware and plan your exit with the utmost forethought and caution. The biggest sin in the eye of the psychopath isn't being useless to her. The biggest sin and threat to the psychopath is knowing her secret. The psychopath spends every waking moment creating a false image of herself to others, an image that includes normal compassion and honesty, and care for the interests of others – the exact opposite of the psychopath's true personality. To know the ugly truth about a psychopath's self-absorption, mercenary motives and deceitfulness is to pose the greatest possible threat to their painstakingly constructed persona.

Though you may be fooled for a time, if you are the sort of person who believes in the basic goodness of your fellow man and are capable of projecting your own good intentions on those around you – and if you can find it tolerable living the entire agenda of the psychopath in your life without complaint – you may find satisfaction, even happiness, living with such a person, at least, for a time. However, it is likely that there will come a time when the psychopath will decide that you no longer offer a suitable cost/benefit, or you will discover a lie or sexual infidelity that will cause you insufferable pain.

And the entire time the psychopath will be sizing up your sympathy and naiveté and calculating how those qualities can be of use to them. As we've described before, in this way the psychopath excels at real empathy (knowing the true feelings of others better than most of us) in contradiction to the psychiatric definition. And she counts this as our weakness and vulnerability. She does not suffer any concern for you and will not sacrifice her desires as a result of sympathy and compassion, but she knows that you may, under the right circumstances.

And here's where the clinical definition of psychopathy comes into play and I can't emphasize enough the difference in personal risk between a relationship with a clinical (PSL-R) psychopath and what I am describing as a Successful Psychopath. While the Successful Psychopath can exercise self-control and avoid outright antisocial and criminal behavior – such as threats, physical assault, even murder – the clinical psychopath will do almost anything, compulsively risking his own freedom and safety, to accomplish his perceived goals. He can't help himself. If you don't have a very complete picture of your psychopath's history, especially any antisocial behaviors, you may have no way of knowing what risk you may face.

In an average lifetime, one is likely to become closely involved with, perhaps, hundreds of people: family, friends, bosses, coworkers, customers, clients and business associates. This could mean knowing a handful of clinical psychopaths. However, as we've described, many clinical psychopaths are institutionalized, either in jail or prison, or psychiatric facilities. And frequently, because of the permanent risk they pose to the public, they are incarcerated for life. But not so with the successful psychopath, which may be as common as one in ten people you meet.

If you suspect that someone in your close circle of loved ones or friends is a psychopath, the most advisable short-term course of action may be to remain constant in your behavior unless and until you are able to find more information to confirm your feelings. In such circumstances, you should privately consult with a qualified mental health professional about your concerns before changing your behavior or taking any action that might reveal what you suspect about this person.

Be sure that you are protected in any possible way from the wrath of the psychopath in your life and avoid revealing what you know about her secret, if at all possible.

Remember, should you become more trouble that you are worth and can't simply be ignored by the psychopath, successful or not, she may still inflict any pain necessary to make you go away; or even simply for revenge and/or the pure pleasure of it.

So the title of this book is both about getting our arms around the frequency of Factor 1 (only) psychopathy, as well as learning to identify the hidden natures of the successful psychopaths in our lives. This is not easy and, with all that's been said about them, one must be very careful about judging who may be a psychopath. Even with full-blown, clinical psychopaths Dr. Hare and many other psychiatric professionals insist that only a qualified mental health-care expert, using the PCL-R and extensive background research and interviews, can make such a diagnosis.

However, the successful psychopath in our life may not be impossible to spot. First of all, you have probably already had significant experience with the suspected empathy-deficient boss, co-worker, family member or (God forbid) spouse. With enough knowledge and exposure to their behaviors, the psychopathic tells become more and more obvious. Certain situations may so obviously call for expressions of empathy, sympathy or remorse that their absence can shock us.

Add other traits of the successful psychopath: superficial glibness and charm, a pattern of deception and manipulation, a sense that they don't feel constrained by the rules (other than to avoid being identified), risk taking, and promiscuousness, and you have the makings of a conclusion about that person. In any event, any combination of those traits should be cause for concern, regardless of whether you may judge that person to be a psychopath.

CHAPTER EIGHT

Successful Psychopaths Throughout History

I know that it may seem impossible to compare the likes of George Bush and Mitt Romney with Genghis Khan and Pol Pot but you should understand by now that the defining feature of the successful psychopath, versus the clinical psychopath, is the ability to roughly comport themselves to the social norms in which they live to avoid unpleasant consequences. In other words, they are able to exercise the calculated self-control that the full-blown psychopath cannot.

And the social norms of the Dark Ages in Eurasia and the Vietnam War era norms of Cambodia are distinctly different (or, at least, somewhat different) for elites than the late 20th and early 21st Century social norms of advanced societies. That's why Khan and Pol Pot are reviled in the here and now, while being functional, even practically successful, in their respective time and place.

In fact, the aim of this chapter is to describe very successful individuals living just within the bounds of the social norms of their time and place, while showing no sign of normal human empathy or remorse for their harmful effect on others. All of the people described in this chapter display those characteristics, no matter what we may think of them. They succeed by virtue of how well they judge what self-serving harm they can get away with and whether their peers accept their actions in real time.

It is difficult to know whether some of the figures described below had anything resembling empathy and remorse as we know it. The norms and expectations for those with power are so corrupt by the standards of today's advanced societies, that it is hard to judge them by those standards. Consider that less than 200 years ago, slavery, depredation and using women and children as virtual chattel was considered acceptable by these same societies. Nevertheless, many more people in history have chosen lives as farmers, artisans, priests, monks, rabbis and nuns that didn't require war, thievery and murder to attain their desires.

Likewise, it is impossible to know for sure whether some of our contemporary political and business elite are Factor 1 psychopaths but, if not, they must have amazing capacities for rationalization to launch bloody wars for resources, political control and pride, or enrich themselves mightily at the expense of the many. And who better to strive for power and status in business and politics and push that power to its limits than someone with a grandiose sense of self, gross egocentrism, and a weak sense of empathy or remorse. A wise man once said, "[y]e shall know them by their fruits. Do men gather grapes of thorns, or figs of thistles? Even so every good tree bringeth forth good fruit; but a corrupt tree bringeth forth evil fruit." – Matthew 7:16-17

***

Caligula

Caligula (12 AD – 41) was born Gaius Julius Caesar Augustus Germanicus in Antium and was initially hailed as a benevolent ruler, son of much-beloved Roman General Germanicus and successor to the much-reviled Emperor Tiberius. He ended then commonplace trials for alleged treason, brought back the exiled, helped those impoverished by imperial taxes, established public accounting and democratic elections, as well as infrastructure and public sporting events.

However, he also spent lavishly, both to buy favor from his patrons and the public and on his own luxurious accommodation, practically bankrupting the state treasury.

After recovering from a serious illness, Caligula had his cousin, adopted son, father-in-law and brother-in-law killed, as well as exiling his two sisters. His enraged Grandmother committed suicide (or was possibly poisoned by Caligula) and he apparently forced one of his helpers to commit suicide as well. Caligula was also criticized for ordering executions without trial and set about a campaign of falsely accusing, fining and sometimes killing wealthier citizens to secure their estates to fill Rome's depleted coffers. Some of the most infamous tales of Caligula's debauchery have been called into question but contemporaneous historians agree that he was egocentric, promiscuous, angry, profligate, killed others on a whim and slept with other men's wives. He erected statues of himself (including in Jewish synagogues and the Temple of Jerusalem) and had Romans, including members of the Roman Senate, worship him as a living god. There is little doubt that Caligula meets the working definition of the successful psychopath: egocentric and charming his way into favor while attempting to mask his lack of empathy toward others and lack of remorse for his harmful actions.

***

Genghis Khan

During the reign of Genghis Khan (born and lived as Temüjin in the late 11th Century in modern-day northern Mongolia), in the early 12th Century, he conquered most of Eurasia (later expanded by his heir Ögedei Khan), marked by wholesale massacres of its civilian populations and soldiers who took up arms against him, and the enslavement of young women and children. In the massacre at Samarkand, Khan raised pyramids of severed heads as a symbol of his conquest, after using African slaves as shields during the siege.

Geneticists, studying Y-chromosome data, have found that nearly 8 percent (or roughly 16 million) of the men in the area of the former Mongol empire carry y-chromosomes that are almost identical.

That is almost 0.5 percent of the male population of the world.

The reason this may well relate to Khan has to do with the sort of "cultural norms" at the time and place of Khan's conquest and rule of the region. They involved the destruction of conquered cities and villages, the slaying of their men and the apportionment of captured females to Khan and his male heirs. It is believed that his eldest son, Tushi, may have had up to 40 sons.

But Khan is also credited with uniting many rival tribes, implementing a rule of law, ruled by meritocracy and is credited with creating the early Silk Road. He was also tolerant of many religions and studied Buddhism, Taoism, Islam and Christianity. Like many successful psychopaths, Khan was ambitious, of a curious mind, persuasive and utterly ruthless in pursuing his ends with little sign of empathy or remorse.

***

Vlad Tepes

Vlad (III) Tepes, Prince of Wallachia, was born to the House of Drăculeşti in Sighişoara, Transylvania, Hungary (now part of Romania) in the early 14th Century, better known as Dracula or Vlad the Impaler, and the inspiration for Bram Stoker's Dracula.

Vlad made his mark (so to speak) as Vlad the Impaler when he slaughtered nearly 1,000 Turkish cavalry in the desire to keep Wallachia from the control of the Ottoman empire and had them impaled on tall stakes. In 1462 he went on to raid Turkish camps in and near Wallachia and kill both soldiers and civilians. Of this campaign he wrote: "I have killed peasants men and women, old and young, who lived at Oblucitza and Novoselo...[w]e killed 23,884 Turks without counting those whom we burned in homes or the Turks whose heads were cut by our soldiers..." That same year he killed 15,000 Turkish troops in a single night and finally drove

Sultan Mehmed II and his remaining army of up to 60,000 out of Wallachia.

The fact that his murderous acts were celebrated among Saxons living in Transylvania, the Italian states and even Pope Pius II, tells you something about the cultural norms of Dark Ages Europe.

It is believed that Vlad III studied combat skills, geography, mathematics, science, the German, Latin and old Slavic languages, as well as classical arts and philosophy. Later, Vlad III would rule his native land of Wallachia, strengthening its agriculture and trade, build new villages for the working class, and support the local Monastery.

So, once again, we see a man of great accomplishment and success, even knowledge and wisdom, who doesn't seem to care in the slightest about the dire, merciless and destructive consequences of his actions.

**

Marquis "Donatien Alphonse François" de Sade

The Marquis de Sade was actually imprisoned and incarcerated in the Charenton insane asylum for a combined 32 years. He was once sentenced to death for sodomy and poisoning prostitutes, sexually abused prostitutes, and was unfaithful with his wife's sister. Many household servants fled from his employ, complaining of sexual abuse by de Sade. He is the namesake for the words sadist, sadism and sadomasochism.

But de Sade was also a prolific novelist, playwright, philosopher, became a Colonel of a Dragoon regiment during the Seven Years War, and was appointed delegate to the National Convention following the French Revolution. He was critical of the bloody Reign of Terror and it has been suggested that his philosophy was a precursor to Socialism, Freudian psychoanalysis, Existentialism and Surrealism, almost two centuries before they were promulgated.

So de Sade was highly intelligent, able to persuade numerous sexual partners into cruel and violent sex acts. Considering his treatment of others over a lifetime, as well as his philosophy, it is hard to imagine that de Sade possessed a great deal of empathy towards others or remorse for the pain he inflicted on them.

***

Adolph Hitler

What really needs to be said about the megalomaniacal psychopathy of Adolph Hitler? Hitler, born on 20 April 1889 in Austria-Hungary near the border with Bavaria, showed an early interest in warfare and the Franco-Prussian War. As a boy he was restless and ran into discipline problems, both at school and at home, particularly after the death of his younger brother when he was 10 years of age. He regularly rebelled against his father, claiming that he intentionally did poorly in school to have his way.

Hitler later adopted both the religious prejudice (particularly anti-Semitism) and racist sentiments that were common in pre-WWI Vienna and then the severe nationalism in the aftermath of Germany's defeat and submission to the rest of Europe. He served in the Bavarian army as a dispatch runner on the Western Front, where he was twice wounded in battle and decorated for bravery by sympathetic superiors. Later he was hospitalized for temporary blindness that he claimed was from British mustard gas, but it is believed that he was dissembling about what may have actually been a case of "hysterical amblyopia" (hysterical blindness).

Despite his lack of academic accomplishment, Hitler proved a charismatic, even mesmerizing speaker based upon the nationalistic politics he practiced in Munich. He quickly crafted a power base in the National Socialist German Workers Party, enlisting allies such as Rudolph Hess and Hermann Göring, eventually launching a failed coup against the Bavarian government. After a short prison term, where he wrote *Mein Kampf* (My Struggle), Hitler was banned from public speaking. Finally, using the pain of the Great Depression to rekindle nationalistic furor, he began his rise to chancellor of the Reichstag and, eventually, de facto dictator of Nazi Germany.

To say that Hitler was ambitious, egocentric, grandiose and ruthless in pursuit of his ambitions, understates the man. He was manifestly bereft of the slightest sympathy toward his victims and remorseful only over his perceived losses. Yet he assembled and led the most powerful military machine the world had ever seen and very nearly conquered all of Europe (while exterminating well over 5 million Jews), mostly by expertly pandering to base motives of his countrymen (empathy indeed). In his day, he was admired, followed, even adored.

***

Joseph Stalin

Joseph Stalin was the all-powerful leader of the Soviet Union, one of the most powerful empires in history, from the mid-1920s until his death in 1953. Born in December of 1878, of a cobbler who became both alcoholic and abusive, Ioseb (Stalin's given name) suffered from a physical birth defect, illness and injury as a child. After being sent to a Greek Orthodox seminary and receiving a scholarship to a Georgian Orthodox seminary, Stalin was expelled, most likely because he couldn't afford the tuition.

Before long, Stalin discovered the writings of Marxist revolutionary Vladimir Lenin, later joining him as Lenin formed the Bolshevics. Like Hitler, Stalin proved an effective leader and motivated his followers with intelligent and compelling propaganda and poetry, along with murderous bank robberies and assassinations of his political opponents. He was arrested and exiled several times, often escaping to become ever more favored by Lenin and evermore powerful. He married twice, his first wife dying of typhus about five years after the birth of Stalin's son.

With Lenin and Leon Trotsky, Stalin helped lead the Russian revolution of 1917 and then suppress the White Army in the Russian Civil War, burning villages and publicly executing army deserters. He continued to build power and a cult of personality as the Soviet Union expanded its control over eastern Europe, establishing intelligence networks across the globe, including pre-WWII Germany (and ultimately defeating the Nazis).

As they say, the rest is history. Again we have an intelligent, educated man with grand ego and ambition who was ready to use any means necessary to achieve his outsized goals, without acting far outside the social norms of his chosen milieu. Stalin was charming and persuasive while also being ruthless, cruel, disloyal, deceptive and remorseless, all to achieve his own selfish ends.

***

George W. Bush

In a way, George W. Bush (and Dick Cheney) may represent the perfect illustration of the successful psychopath working the boundaries of sociopathic behavior in the modern era. You can't get much more successful than rising to the level of President, after governing one of the largest states in the union, even if while riding the coattails of a former president father.

At the same time, this power was mightily abused for their own purposes, political and otherwise. Deceiving the public, the Congress, and our allies abroad into supporting a preemptive, unnecessary and ill-conceived war, based upon false and often fabricated pretenses, is perhaps the most immoral choice a president can make. Add war crimes such as torture, using techniques developed during the Spanish Inquisition and used by both the Japanese and Germans on American soldiers during WWII, and you see a level of antisocial orientation that shocks the conscious of those with more typical morality.

Dr. Justin Frank published the book, *Bush on the Couch*, a study of Bush's history and conduct that concluded that he was probably a psychopath. Frank traces Bush's possible psychopathy from his experience as a young boy, raised by an absent, patrician father and a stern withholding mother, who disallowed mourning the death of Bush's beloved younger sister. He is known to have tortured animals, a red flag for a psychopathic personality after a certain age. And surely, few people have been as arrogantly unapologetic (unable to even utter the words "shame on me") and cock-sure of their morally bankrupt conduct.

Yet the former president (and his enablers) have to date faced no punishment whatsoever (other than disapproval, even disgust, by great swaths of the public throughout the world). Even those who despise the Bush Administration's conduct have, more or less acquiesced to the fact that it is politically untenable to hold them accountable in any concrete way. Even though President Bush and Dick Cheney are virtual prisoners within their own country for fear of arrest for war crimes by other western nations, they are often treated as though they have comported themselves within normal bounds.

***

Richard "Dick" Cheney

Before ignoring the Al Qaeda threat, the launching of a torture program that was well-known to be almost useless for revealing any actionable intelligence (but very useful in extracting any desired false confession) and lying the country into a bloody, unnecessary war, Dick Cheney was the chairman and CEO of Halliburton, one of the world's largest oil development firms and parent company of Kellogg-Brown & Root. As Defense Secretary, Cheney had approved a study by Brown & Root on the use of private military forces with American soldiers in combat, to the tune of over $8.5 million.

Halliburton and its subsidiaries, particularly KBR, violated trade rules by selling certain equipment to the then embargoed countries of Iraq and Libya, was fined for dealing with the Libyan government, caused oil spills and toxic chemical releases and, while under Cheney's direction, did business with Iran through its foreign offices. It was accused of receiving $billions in no-bid government contracts and paid fines and settlements of three-quarters of a $billion for bribing foreign officials. Cheney left the company in 2000 with a severance package worth $36 million.

Later, during the Cheney vice presidency the Bush Administration contracted with Halliburton while Cheney was receiving hundreds of thousands of dollars in deferred compensation. KBR was responsible for building sub-standard military bases in Iraq that electrocuted US soldiers and causing the Deep Water Horizon oil rig explosion, resulting in the Gulf Oil Spill, and later plead guilty to destroying evidence related to the spill. We'll leave future history to judge Cheney for being a huge force in continued fossil fuel production and use, which he must know kills untold numbers of wildlife, threatens entire species and may ultimately doom human civilization, as we have known it.

It's fair to say that Cheney was quite successful in both business and government while leaving death, destruction and corruption in his wake. Cheney's arrogance is both infamous and shameless and he has never shown the slightest remorse for the massive pain and destruction he has caused. In February 2006, Cheney famously shot an acquaintance in the face, neck, and chest during a controlled quail hunt, giving him a heart attack and a collapsed lung. Cheney admitted to drinking "one beer" before the incident and was said to be drinking and laughing about it shortly thereafter. He was shielded from interviews with local authorities for almost two days, about the time that the news was released to the press. The shooting victim later apologized, saying he was "deeply sorry" for what he had put Cheney and his family through.

***

Willard "Mitt" Romney

Mitt Romney, before he became Governor of Massachusetts and a perennial presidential candidate, made a fortune as cofounder, president and managing general partner of Bain Capital. The exact purpose of a venture capital/private equity company is to maximize the value of acquired companies and returns to the venture capital company's investors. In the capitalist system, fiduciary responsibility requires it. Bain and Romney profited from leveraged buyouts; buying companies with borrowed money, inflating their balance sheets, extracting large management fees and then selling those companies at the peak of their market value, leaving them saddled with the debt Bain had borrowed, often leading to layoffs and bankruptcy.

As governor, Romney reversed himself to oppose civil unions for gay couples and a woman's right to choose, finally vetoing legislation to expand access to emergency contraception as well as embryonic stem cell research. Later, while preparing for and campaigning for the 2012 presidential campaign, Romney moved ever more rightward on proposed policy, refused to release his tax returns (as all recent presidential candidates had done), finally revealing his notion that "47%" of Americans were essentially freeloaders (at least they didn't generally destroy lives and livelihoods and park their money in foreign banks to avoid taxes).

One famous incident offers a revealing window into Romney's lack of compassion for the helpless. It seems that Romney ran out of room in the car while packing for a family vacation, starting with a 12-hour drive at highway speeds. Romney elected to place the family Irish Setter, Seamus, in a carrier on the roof of the car to make more room. Obviously, most dog owners would recoil in shock at such an idea, but for Gov. Romney it was simply a matter of practical expediency. Seamus eventually developed diarrhea and shat himself and the car roof and back window during the trip. Romney later claimed that Seamus "enjoyed himself," during the ride. He ran off (Seamus, not Romney) when they reached their destination in Canada.

Although Romney's conduct is of an order less destructive than those listed before him, and nothing approaching the socio-pathic conduct that marks the PCL-R psy-chopath, he nevertheless exemplifies the successful psychopathy of our modern cap-italist system. No harm done to others is considered amoral as long as it can be de-scribed as profitable success. In Romney's case, the "creative" destruction of busi-nesses and livelihoods is actually counted as a legally sanctioned (even necessary) good in this economic system, at least among those who practice within it and their supporters. Many, as evidenced by Romney's 2012 presidential election bid, may feel otherwise.

***

The Psychopath in Your Life

There are probably thousands, even millions of successful psychopaths who have
helped shape the societies in which they
lived, mostly for the worse. The psychopaths described above are remarkable in
their outsized accomplishment. The successful (or otherwise) psychopaths in your
life may have also been as remarkable in
their inability to feel for others as we do,
even without ruling countries or societies
according to their ambitions. They are also
remarkable in the fact that we often seem
blind to their psychological differences, no
matter what harm they do to the rest of us.

We can almost understand why when we
consider that psychopathy was only (barely) recognized as a psychological condition
in the mid twentieth century. Experts in the
field still insist that a history of sociopathic
behavior beyond what has been described
above must be present to meet the definition of true psychopathy. And, to this day,
the psychological profession refuses to call

even full-blown clinical psychopathy a disorder. But you have been warned and, by now, probably know better.

Psychopathy or "Mere" Rationalization?

I realize now that I should have written more about rationalization and her twin sister: denial. It is important enough in the context of recognizing the successful psychopath that a book revision was in order.

Rationalization and denial are mental processes we all engage in fairly often, which allow us to do or say that which we might otherwise think incorrect, unwise or improper. By contrast, Factor 1 psychopathy, unlike mere rationalization, is a fairly rare yet lifelong and irredeemable gross egocentrism, conning manipulativeness, and a distinct lack of empathy or remorse for harm done to others.

Most of the things we rationalize are pretty mundane, why we should neglect some undesirable chore for the time being for some invented reason, being one typical example. Or simply in support of some belief about people or things which fit our pre-existing prejudices and/or psychology. But some of the things we say or do by the process of rationalization can be quite profound. It is not hyperbole to say that the rationalization process allowed for Nazism, what turned the better part of a nation of otherwise peaceful, moral human beings into murderous, even genocidal monsters. This occurs in nearly all wars, by any nation, by normal people.

It is what allowed Stanley Milgram's study volunteers (see *Milgram Experiment*) to inflict what they believed was tremendous pain, even potential death, on subjects merely because they were instructed to do so by authority figures in lab coats. It is the process by which the fake Stanford prison guards (see *Stanford Prison Experiment*) became sadistic torturers merely through peer pressure and unrestricted authority. It allows child molesters and rapists to give license to their compulsions, and allows terrorists to commit mass murder of innocents. But it is not usually unremorseful psychopathy, nor is the darkest side of it very common.

The motive behind much of this undesirable (and subconsciously undesired) behavior and rationalization is simple fear. From fear of opprobrium (often in the form of peer pressure) to fear of punishment, many of us decide some of our behavior and beliefs from these fears. In *The Authoritarians*, Dr. Bob Altemeyer attempts to quantify the numbers of us who are susceptible to this sort of fear-based decision-making – which tends to agree with the numbers seen in the Milgram and Stanford experiments, as well as other analyses – and the personality behind this thinking and behavior. His studies were political-based, so he coined his fear-reactive personality "High RWA (Right-Wing-Authoritarian-Following)." The personality he describes has been scarred from childhood to believe (perhaps not incorrectly) that the surrounding world is a dangerous and scary place and that a strong, authoritarian ("Daddy-like") figure should be followed and obeyed to be protected from it.

Yet non-psychopaths who do or say inhumane things still often suffer personal trauma and psychological consequences for their actions. Many times, permanent psychological suffering of some sort from the mostly repressed, sub-conscious memories of what they have done. Many soldiers suffer post-traumatic stress disorder (PTSD), and not only those who are injured in battle. Many otherwise perfectly unscathed former soldiers can suffer from PTSD, which can include severe anxiety disorders, depression and even result in suicide, merely from what they have witnessed.

Currently, US drone controllers, who are ordered to fire missiles at so-called "enemy-combatants" from air-conditioned rooms, thousands of miles from battle or their victims, are falling victim themselves to severe stress disorders. Their victims can be anyone from actual violent, armed militants to innocent women and children; entire wedding parties have on occasion been blown to bits. Servicemen who witness some of the carnage they inflict turn to drugs and alcohol abuse to try to self-medicate their psychological trauma. Some kill themselves. These are not psychopaths, they are merely normal human beings who are pressured to and rationalize acts that shock their own consciences.

Studies show that, under certain authority, peer pressures, and circumstances, only about 15-25% of us are able to resist committing awful, immoral acts upon others. The rest of

us will do what we are coerced to do and suffer for it. Only the 10% or more of those who
do not resist *or regret* committing such may-
hem on others are the true psychopaths. In
some ways, the Successful Psychopath, the
one who lives an apparently normal, produc-
tive life thereafter, is the scariest creature of
all. The successful psychopath may sometimes
indeed engage in rationalization and, certainly, denial. But so do others, on a regular basis.

And their rationalizations may allow them to
be every bit as inhumane and dangerous to us
as any psychopath. Their empathy and remorse is simply buried and buried completely
for the purpose of the harm they may inflict
upon someone. If 1-2% of a given sample
group of people meet the definition of clinical
(often criminal) psychopathy and another 10%
are successful psychopaths – successful at hiding their constant egocentrism, conning manipulation and lack of empathy or remorse,
through greater self control over their rule-
breaking impulses – those who are capable of
rationalizing harm to themselves or to others
comprise a frightening number of the rest of
us.

Denial is also a mental process where we pretend that something we did or said (or even something that occurs without our doing) that we find unconscionable, didn't really happen. We create a mythical history in which it did not occur, at least not in its true form. As was pointed out previously, we have an unparalleled ability to perceive the objective reality of the world around us and what we make of it, matched by an unbridled ability to alter that perception and our memory of that reality.

So, for practical purposes, the relevance of psychopathy to your relationships to others is almost secondary to all of the possible motives of the more common and ordinary people who surround you. This is not a suggestion that you remain unaware of the psychopathic features of those with whom you deal, or to be paranoid or even unwilling to trust anyone, but a strong recommendation against blind trust and investing heavily in anyone you don't think you know well enough to trust.

Primarily, don't be fooled by apparent niceness. Almost anyone can fake niceness, even considerateness, at least for a time. Psychopaths can fake apparent niceness, hour after

hour, day after day, week after week, year after year, as long as it serves their purposes. Even a child can do it.

It is when people are at their worst, that they reveal their true selves. A man who can be physically or emotionally abusing, even for a moment, is showing you something about his nature. Remember, even full-blown, clinical, criminal psychopaths regularly fool trained psychologists with their charm and intelligence, until enough time is spent with them to reveal something very dark and troubling. The "tell" for psychopathy is a consistent or repeated behavior demonstrating little or no empathy for the suffering of others and little or no remorse for any harm they do to others. This may occur even as they appear to be normal, charming, even nice people.

But, take heart. It appears that something like 25-30% of people have a magnificent sense of empathy, morality and ethical behavior, enough to sacrifice themselves to adhere to their own sense of right and wrong. Others, up to the psychopathic 10% (another 60-65% of us) live on a spectrum of morality and ethics, many capable of self-sacrifice and heroism. Most of us can, for the most part, be trusted much of the time (sorry for necessary multiple qualifiers).

However, unlike psychopathy, which can become predictable if the signs are observed and recognized, rationalized harmful behavior can happen without very much warning, even by people who may seem to have an otherwise normal sense of empathy. I hope that this explanation of these difficult facets of human personality: psychopathic features and the power of rationalization and defensive denial make you as careful in your investment in others as they should. The proverb *"fools rush in where angels fear to tread,"* (attributed to Alexander Pope from his poem *"An Essay on Criticism,"* 1709), is actually a critique of much of his day's artistic criticism (as the title suggests) but it is often taken as a comment on heroism. But, when it comes to committing to a relationship it is often quite the opposite.

It is the good hearts and dependably moral human beings who often project those attributes on others and make tragic mistakes regarding who they may stake their happiness upon. It is terribly important to take a hard, unbiased examination of the actions of those who we are attracted to (or must deal with in everyday life) and use that inventory to try to determine their moral underpinnings and our response to them. People, who by their everyday behavior, are obviously selfless, giving, caring, and honestly other-focused, are usually what they seem to be. Likewise, those who, even on occasion, seem selfish or mean-spirited in their behavior should be taken at face value. These attributes come from somewhere in that person and are usually telling about what lies at the center of their being.

Regardless, whether unremorseful psychopath or sub-conscious rationalizer, those who inflict serious harm on others need not be outright killers or child-rapists. They can be lovers, family, friends, public officials (or your average voter), bosses, or captains of industry. Their choices may destroy individual lives, social economies, animal species, even global ecosystems or entire civilizations. From a practical perspective, either the mechanisms of unremorseful psychopathic personality or repressed rationalization and denial, can be equally dangerous for any or all of us.